INDIAN WORKERS ASSOCIATION (SOUTHALL)

bharti mazdoor sabha

60 YEARS OF STRUGGLES AND ACHIEVEMENTS 1956-2016

BY BALRAJ PUREWAL

APPEAL

It is our intention to produce a second edition of this book as we believe that there exists a wealth of untapped additional information, photographs and other materials within our community that should be shared with or made available to the wider public.

We appeal to anyone who may have any information, photographs, film footage or any other materials to contact us so we may amend or update existing information or make new information available on the history of the Indian Workers' Association (Southall).

Please help us record and preserve the heritage and history of the IWA (Southall) for future generations.

If you have any information, photographs, film footage or any other materials connected to the IWA, please contact:
Balraj Purewal
email: director@taha.org.uk
Tel: 0788 2537336

All rights reserved. No part of this publication may be reproduced, stored in a retrieval system, or transmitted in any form or by any means, electronic, mechanical, photocopying, recording or otherwise, without the prior written consent of the copyright owner.

All enquiries regarding any extracts or re-use of any material in this book should be addressed to the copyright owner, Balraj Purewal.

Published by The Asian Health Agency

© Balraj Purewal 2016

We acknowledge support from Southall Travel

FOREWORD

This book is dedicated to the early pioneers and immigrants from the Panjab region of India who came to Britain in the 1950s and who established the Indian Workers' Association (IWA) in Southall in 1956 to address problems facing these newly arriving immigrants and to support them to integrate into the host community.

These early pioneers who founded IWA originated from rural and agricultural backgrounds and primarily from villages in the Doaba and surrounding regions. On arrivals in Britain they faced appalling housing and harsh employment conditions, working in the lowest paid, unsafe, dirty and manual jobs. Their situation and plight was further exasperated by having to adjust to a totally different environment and cultural norms, with little or no knowledge of English and subjected to overt racial discrimination which they had to endure in almost every sphere of their daily living. These pioneers and their predecessors gave their all to their kith, kin and community, organising themselves to create the IWA, an organisation based on secular values.

One of the greatest achievements of the IWA was its ability to translate and embed the concept of *'SEVA - serving the community',* commitments to secular values and community self-help into reality within the thinking and working of the IWA. The fact that IWA was and continues to be an independent self-sustaining organisation to this day, providing free advice and welfare support to thousands of people every year, is a testimony to the values on which the pioneers founded the organisation.

It is also dedicated to those who served as members of the IWA Executive Committee over 6 decades and countless active rank and file members who worked and campaigned tirelessly for basic human dignity and rights and to protect our communities. Together they ensured that their children and future generations could have a better future, be treated as equal citizens in their new home and not face the indignities, discrimination, inequality and racism that they themselves had to suffer and endure.

The IWA's immense contribution to challenging unjust and unfair immigration controls, promoting anti-discriminatory legislation and good race relations, inspiring a generation of black and Asian community leaders into community leadership roles and mainstream politics, particularly during the 1960s and 1970s, is unparalleled.

I am indebted to the founding fathers of IWA and the early pioneers whose sacrifices, struggles and contribution ensured a fairer and better future for us all. On behalf of myself and our community, I feel privileged to have known many of them and to be able to pay a tribute to our unsung heroes.

Balraj Singh Purewal
Chief Executive, TAHA
IWA Assistant General Secretary, 1983-1994
General Secretary, 1986-1987.

ABOUT THE AUTHOR

BALRAJ PUREWAL

For many local residents in Southall, Balraj Purewal is an unsung hero. From the mid 1970s he was one of the key leaders and spokesperson of the Southall Youth Movement (SYM), an organisation baptised by the murderous intent of racism that took the life of young Gurdip Singh Chaggar on the streets of Southall in June 1976. The discrimination and racism that Purewal experienced on the street, at school and in the sports arena, along with other people of his generation, was to have a profound impact and influence on his life. He remains one of the very few persons from West London, who continues to expose the damaging impact of State and institutional racism.

Purewal was born in Jassowal, Hoshiarpur, in Punjab on 3rd April 1954 and came to Britain in December 1961 at the age of 8 with his family and lived at 69 Woodlands Road, Southall. As a young Sikh boy, Balraj had to have his hair cut and become a 'Mona' Sikh as part of an effort to assimilate into British society.

Purewal went to Beaconsfield Primary School but was transferred to Tudor Road Primary School after about 6 months as a consequence of a discriminatory policy of 'dispersal' or 'bussing' of immigrant children. He completed his secondary school education at Dormers Wells High School.

Purewal and SYM was one of the key centrifugal forces to mobilise continually from 1976 to 1981, when over 30 English cities suffered serious public order disturbances caused by racial tension and policing of black and Asian communities. Locally the Asian community felt vulnerable to racial violence, the growth of the far right and police indifference or hostility. Although Chaggar's murder on 4 June 1976 had lit the spark for youth mobilisation, community spirit was severely tested by the gravity of Blair Peach's murder in spring 1979 and the burning of Hamborough Tavern, both caused by the dangerous presence of the far right on Southall's doorstep. I remember the SYM in action during that period. It was fearless and brave and was uncompromising in the face of adversity no matter how great the odds. Purewal was its General Secretary from 1976 until 1983. Although the movement was short-lived it gave a powerful independent voice to hundreds of young Asians in west London, and inspired thousands of others across Britain. Regardless of its shortcomings, at its peak it can only be described as a rough diamond forged by local conditions that others tried to chisel in their own image but never succeeded.

Purewal was the only youth leader who made the leap from the politics of young people to immersing himself in Indian Workers' Association (IWA) of Southall, an organisation initially representing workers and then community, including business, interests locally. He initially stood in the IWA elections in 1979 but was elected to its Executive Committee in 1983 a member of an alliance called Allied United Front that was led by Piara Singh Khabra and Tarsem Singh Toor. For decades, both Khabra and Toor were formidable operators within Britain's Panjabi community nationally. Khabra became the first Asian Labour MP to be elected from Southall's generation of community leaders to represent the local constituency, and Purewal was one of the key drivers to ensure his success both during the nomination process and at the elections. Toor's political ambitions ended when he was tragically assassinated in January 1986 for political reasons and his killing still remains unsolved. Purewal resigned from the IWA in 1994. He had high ambition for this powerful organisation but sometimes it was burdened by its own history.

Purewal's first attempt to document the history of the IWA has to be applauded for many reasons not least because he has created a new beacon for social historians. The sad fact is that Southall social history, including the enormous struggles for equality waged by newcomers to the area, has never been documented properly especially by people who made history in that period. This booklet needs to be read and digested for the right reasons and others need to take the baton to complete the mission.

Suresh Grover
Director
The Monitoring Group

CONTENTS

SECTION 1   9
   Immigration Controls   10
   The Panjab and Doaba Connection   12
   Aldgate East London to Southall   16
   Shepherds Bush Gurdwara   18
   New and Old Southall   20
   Early Arrivals and Panjabi Settlements in Southall   22
   Establishment of Sri Guru Singh Sabha Southall   24
   Early Indian Businesses in Southall   26
   Sikhs and Racial Discrimination   30
   Communal Living and Support Networks   34
   Racism in Employment   36
   Racism and Trade Unions   38
   Discrimination in Housing   40
   Social and Cultural Life in the 1950s and 60s   42
   Sports   50

SECTION 2   53
   The IWAs in Britain in the 1900s: Fighting for Indian Independence   54
   Formation of IWA Southall: 1956   58
   IWA Aims and Objects   64

SECTION 3   67
   Indians and Irregular Immigration Status   68
   Early Immigrants and Tax Claims   69
   Strike at Rockware Glass: Greenford   70
   Dura Tube & Wire Ltd Strike   72
   The R. Woolfe's Rubber Factory   74
   Dispersal and Bussing of Asian schoolchildren in Southall   78
   Dominion Cinema: The Golden Years   82
   Demise of the Dominion Cinema   86
   IWA Welfare Services   90
   Indian Passport and Visa Service   95
   Virginity Tests on Asian women from Indian sub-continent at Heathrow Airport   96
   Murder of Chaggar: 4th June 1976   98
   National Front Meeting in Southall Town Hall: The Murder of Blair Peach   100
   IWA and Public Funding   104

IWA Anti-Racism Training Programmes and Publications	106
National and International Work and Campaigns	108

SECTION 4 — 117

- IWA: Membership — 118
- Executive Committee Structure — 120
- Annual General Meetings — 122
- Internal Factions and Alliances — 126
- Elections — 130
- Active Opposition and Disputes — 134
- IWA Presidents and General Secretaries: 1956 - 2016 — 136
- Profile of IWA Presidents and General Secretaries: 1956-2016 — 137
  - Presidents — 137
  - General Secretaries — 139
  - IWA Welfare Officers — 141
  - Longest Serving IWA Member — 141

SECTION 5 — 143

- Breaking the Glass Barriers: From IWA to Mainstream Politics — 144
- IWA and Labour Party Connection — 144
- Sardul Gill: First Elected Asian Councillor in Ealing, May 1968 — 148
- Vishnu Sharma: The Independent Candidate, 1973 Council Elections — 148
- Piara Khabra: First Asian Member of Parliament for Southall/Ealing — 149
- IWA Executive Committee members who became Councillors — 150
- IWA: The Legacy — 152

SECTION 6 — 155

- Key milestones in the history of IWA — 156

ACKNOWLEDGEMENTS — 159

REFERENCES — 160

- Photographs — 160

SECTION 1

This section summarises some of the main issues which inform or are relevant to an understanding of the backgrounds and experiences of the early immigrants from the Indian Sub-continent as well as the development of the Indian community and the Indian Workers' Association in Southall.

IMMIGRATION CONTROLS

After World War II, Britain had an open door immigration policy and actively recruited and encouraged migrant workers from their former colonies to come to Britain to meet its insatiable demand for labour to rebuild its infrastructure and reinvigorate its economy. Britain needed labour to run its factories, foundries, transport, build infrastructure, National Health Service et al and looked to migrant workers from the Commonwealth and Pakistan to fill low paid manual jobs that British workers did not want to do.

The 1948 British Nationality Act created the status of Citizen of the UK and Colonies and under this legislation, citizens from Commonwealth countries were free to enter the UK without any restriction. The term 'British' or 'Commonwealth citizen' were and meant the same thing.

However, by the early 1960s and in response to the rising concerns and hostility towards the increasing numbers of immigrants coming from the Commonwealth countries, the British Government introduced the Commonwealth Immigration Act 1962, imposing immigration controls and introduced a voucher system for Commonwealth citizens.

The Commonwealth Immigrants Act of 1968 defined UK citizens solely in terms of citizens who were born, adopted, registered or naturalised in the UK or who had such a parent or grandparent. This new definition acted to impose further controls on immigrants from 'black' Commonwealth countries such as India and Bangladesh as well as Pakistan as opposed to those from 'white' Commonwealth countries such as Australia, Canada or New Zealand.

Further restrictions were imposed to curb immigration from the Commonwealth countries. The Immigration Act 1971, separated migrants into 'patrials' (those who had a link with a British born person) and 'non patrials' (those who did not have any links with a British born person). 'Non Patrials' could only enter and 'live, work and settle in the UK by permission'.

Under this 1971 Act, the voucher system was also replaced by a renewable work permit, valid for 4 years, which meant that work permit holders only had rights to settlement after 4 years. This effectively put a stop to new migrant workers from the Commonwealth settling in the UK. The majority of immigrants accepted for settlement after this were the wives, children and parents of those who had already entered the UK before the introduction of the Immigration Act 1971 which came into effect on 1 January 1973.

The British Nationality Act 1981, further acted to restrict the right of 'non patrials' to work or live in the UK.

Over the decades the IWA lobbied successive governments and campaigned vigorously for the regularisation of illegal immigrants and against unfair and racist immigration laws. Its national campaigning contributed to the Government announcing an Amnesty for Commonwealth citizens and citizens of Pakistan who entered illegally on or after 9 March 1968 and before 1 January 1973.

Sikhs demonstrating against racist Immigration laws (Surjit Bilga 1st Left)

New arrivals at Heathrow airport before Immigration Act 1968

THE PANJAB AND DOABA CONNECTION

The majority of early immigrants who came to settle in Southall originated primarily from Panjab (Land of the Five Rivers) and from farming backgrounds predominately from villages within the Doaba ('Do' meaning 'Two' and 'Ab' meaning 'River': Persian) region situated between the two Rivers of Satluj and Beas.

The Doaba region comprises the districts of Hoshiarpur, Jalandhar, Nawanshahar and Karpurthala and most of the first wave of immigrants came particularly from the Hoshiarpur and Jalandhar districts.

Malwa and Majha constituted the other regions of Panjab. Malwa, the biggest region of Panjab includes the districts of Ludhiana, Bhatinda, Mohali, Sangrur and Patiala and Majha region includes Amritsar, Pathankot, Gurdaspur and Taran Tarn districts.

In order to secure the relevant documentation essential to their entry into Britain, the early Panjabi immigrants engaged the services of 'agents', namely Gian Chand based in Hoshiarpur and Kewal Singh (of Kurkar village) and Chanan Singh (of Chichi village) in Jalandhar. The other agents included Kapil Dev (of Shankar) and Roop Lal (of Banga).

Gian Chand is reputed and accredited with assisting hundreds if not thousands of Panjabis to gain the necessary documentation for entry into Britain. Gian Chand acquired an unenviable reputation amongst those that came or aspired to come to England for his expertise and generosity and in innumerable cases facilitated the entry of Panjabis without charge; asking them to send him his fees as soon as they had gained employment or established themselves in the UK.

In the 1950s, landholdings amongst Panjabis was becoming small with the increasing division and sharing of land within families. Additionally many Panjabi refugees who had been dislocated as a consequence of the partition of India by the British in 1947 and arrived in India were under severe economic pressure to survive. These factors along with a struggling economy in India, after its independence, contributed to the pressure on Panjabis to emigrate.

During the 1950s, Panjabis had to raise Rs/4,000 to come to Britain, often by selling or taking loans against their ancestral or family land. The currency in India at the time comprised of Rupees; with 4 Paisas in 1 Anna, 16 Annas (64 Pasias) in 1 Rupee. In 1964 decimalisation was introduced and resulted in there being 100 Paisas in 1 Rupee.

In the 1950s, one English pound was worth about 13 Indian Rupees and its value fluctuated between 13 to 16 rupees through the 1950s and 1960s.

In the 1950s, an acre of agricultural land in Panjab was estimated to be worth around Rs/6,000. The same land in 2016 is valued at around Rs/250,000, almost equivalent to £25,000.

There was no British Consulate in Panjab at that time and Panjabis had to travel to Simla where the British Consulate was located to apply for and get visas to come to Britain. Emigration from Panjab into Britain, particularly from rural areas, was specifically discouraged by Jawarlal Nehru's Indian government which did not want to project a negative image of India abroad.

It was easier for educated and professional Indians to get visas for Britain. The less well educated and those from rural and farming backgrounds had to circumvent this problem by first getting visas to places like Singapore, which were easier to obtain, and from there obtain a visa

Map of Panjab and its Districts

to enter Britain as these places were British colonies and there were no restrictions on people travelling to Britain.

Since its formation in 1956, many of the IWA's leading figures and officers have originated from the Doaba region and from villages within Jalandhar or Hoshiarpur districts.

'Most of them in the beginning until 1963 were from rural areas of Panjab. Naturally they were not rich peasants'.
Vishnu Dutt Sharma

IWA protest against Immigration Act in central London, 1971

ALDGATE EAST LONDON TO SOUTHALL

Many of the early Indians to the UK had come by sea through various ports including London Tilbury Docks and settled in the East London particularly in and around the Aldgate area. By 1950 there was a small but established Panjabi community in and around the Aldgate area of East London as well as around Shepherds Bush where the first Sikh Gurdwara was situated. During this period many Panjabis were working as 'pedlars' licensed for and involved in 'door to door' selling of goods and as such self-employed. Self employment was preferred by many of the early settlers as it often generated more income than working in harsh and low paid jobs along with more independence.

Many Panjabi immigrants commuted from Aldgate and East London areas to Southall due to the ready availability of work at factories in the area and particularly at the R. Woolfe's Rubber Factory on the border of Southall and Hayes. This Rubber Factory, as it was commonly known, had developed a reputation for providing almost guaranteed employment to Panjabis and particularly Sikhs. This reputation had been promoted by Mr. Dunn, one of its General Managers, an ex-serviceman who had served in British Army in India with a Sikh battalion and held an admiration of Panjabis as being honest and hard working people. The employment of Giani Maher Singh, who had served in the same battalion as the General Manager, acted to attract and increase the recruitment of Panjabis into the Rubber factory which increasingly needed labour to fill manual jobs that white workers were no longer prepared to do, found hard or dirty. Giani Maher Singh had come from 'Bar' region and is known to be one of the first Panjabi Sikhs to be employed at the Rubber factory. This factory became popular and synonymous with employing newly arriving Indians as well as Pakistanis.

The daily journey and commuting from Aldgate East to Southall was difficult given that many of the early immigrants could not speak English, used to take a long time by public transport with the train and bus fares being high. These factors combined to encourage these Indians to consider settling in Southall and consequently they began renting and purchasing property in Southall.

The early Panjabis who moved from Aldgate to Southall included Jarnail Singh Hura, Fakir Singh ('Fikiria') and Pritam Singh Sangha ('Bhai'), who also worked at the Rubber factory and later set up some of the first Indian businesses in Southall.

Numerous cases provide anecdotal evidence of Indians arriving in Southall or landing at Heathrow airport in the morning and starting employment at the Rubber factory on that very same afternoon until the early 1960s.

Naranjan Singh Binning's clothing shop at 9 Artillery Lane East London, an area associated with Sikh settlers from the 1930s.

SHEPHERDS BUSH GURDWARA

The first Gurdwara in London was established in Putney in 1911 by the Khalsa Jatha: British Isles (London) which itself was set up in 1908. In 1913, this Gurdwara was moved to 79 Sinclair Road, London W14 0NJ, a Georgian 3 storey terraced house following a donation made by Maharaja Bhupinder Singh of Patiala. This Gurdwara was initially known as Bhupinder Dharmsala as a tribute to and in recognition of the support given by the Maharaja of Patiala.

The Gurdwara known as 'Shepherds Bush' Gurdwara held weekly Diwans in 1953 and in 1954 it appointed a full-time Granthi (Priest).

This Gurdwara was an integral part of the 'journey' of many early Indian immigrants, particularly Panjabi Sikhs, arriving in Britain in the 1950s. It provided temporary accommodation and refuge to those who did not have any relatives or friends to go to and those who were in 'transit' between one town to another.

Shaheed Udham Singh, whose father was murdered in the Jallianwala massacre in Amritsar on 13 April 1919 by General Reginald Dyer and who later shot General Dyer in Caxton Hall, London and subsequently hanged, is reputed to have stayed at this Gurdwara.

There was no Gurdwara in Southall in the 1950s and the Shepherds Bush Gurdwara played a prominent part in the lives of Sikhs by providing a place of worship and acting as the 'community hub' providing space for all Indians to come together, network and secure support. The Gurdwara building comprised of a large 3 storey terraced house, with the kitchen area on the ground floor, the Gurdwara prayer area on the first floor and accommodation consisting of 4-5 rooms on the third floor.

The Sinclair Road Gurdwara played a critical part in supporting the early Indians and as such holds a special place amongst the early immigrants who came to Britain in the 1950s and particularly amongst those Sikhs who settled in Southall, London, Gravesend and surrounding areas.

In 1969, the Khalsa Jatha sold the Sinclair Road Gurdwara building and purchased another building known as Norland Castle on Queensland Road, where the current Shepherds Bush Gurdwara stands.

Thousands of Sikh immigrants to the UK who settled in London and the Midlands from the 1930s onwards can trace their arrival to the Shepherds Bush Gurdwara directly or indirectly.

Surjit Singh Bilga addressing a Sikh community meeting at Featherstone School Hall, 1962

Exhibition of collection of weapons of Guru Gobind Singh Ji at India House, Aldwych, London.

NEW AND OLD SOUTHALL

Southall basically consisted of Southall and Old ('Purana': Panjabi for 'old') Southall with the railway line and railway bridge acting as the dividing line between these two parts. House prices and rented accommodation in Old Southall being relatively cheaper comparative to that in 'new Southall'.

Trolley buses powered by overhead electricity cables operated on The Broadway until 1962 when they were replaced by motor buses. These open door double decker motor buses were manned by a driver and a conductor.

From 1936 until 1960, a trolleybus (route 607) powered by overhead electric cables operated on the route between Uxbridge and Shepherds Bush including along The Broadway, Southall. Route 207 was introduced on 9 November 1960 and the trolleybuses were replaced by motor buses and operated by a crew of 2, a driver and a conductor who collected fares and issued tickets. In 1987 a one man crew was introduced and in the 1990, the limited stops bus Route 607 began, paralleling Route 207.

The early Indian population was mainly located in the 'new' part of Southall and particularly around the streets currently within the Northcote and The Broadway ward areas and nearby streets. This was attributed to a number of factors including proximity to the Rubber factory and easy access to transport links. The first Indian businesses also sprang up in this area, firstly on or around Beaconsfield Road and later on The Broadway.

The dominance of 'new' Southall over 'Purana' Southall continued throughout the decades, with the main Asian businesses being set up along The Broadway and it becoming established as the main shopping area in Southall. Over the years, The Broadway, Southall developed a national reputation and became known as one of the premiere Asian shopping streets in the country.

This perception and distinction remained until the 1970s when established and prosperous Indians and others began settling in the Norwood Green area of 'Purana' Southall giving it the 'affluent' area people today associate with this particular part of Southall.

Southall Town Hall, 1960s

The Broadway, 1970s

EARLY ARRIVALS AND PANJABI SETTLEMENTS IN SOUTHALL

One of the first known Panjabi families to settle in Southall were 3 brothers, Charan Singh Bilga, Jagar Singh Bilga and Lave Singh Bilga who in 1938 lived at 64 Woodlands Road and later on purchased 66 Woodlands Road.

After Indian Independence in 1947 and prior to 1950 there were very few Panjabis in Southall and most of the Panjabis lived in Aldgate East (London) area. Information and accounts from local elders confirm that during the 1950s, there was a growing number of Panjabis settling in Southall. Two Panjabis that feature and play a prominent role in Panjabi settlement and history in Southall were Pritam Singh Sangha ('Bhai') and Fakir Singh ('Fikiria'), who originally had lived in Aldgate East but relocated to Southall in 1950 and are associated with setting up the first known business in Southall.

Pritam Singh Sangha in partnership with his friend and business associate, Jarnail Singh Hura (also known as 'Ghura'), established the first known business in Southall and Fakir Singh purchased numerous houses which he rented out to his countrymen.

Between 1950 and 1956 when the IWA was established, a number of Panjabis have been identified as living in Southall.

1950
Menga Singh (Lambardar) from Rurka
Jarnail Singh Ghura who came to England on 14 Nov 1950, initially stayed in Birmingham and moved in Southall (and later in partnership with Jagir Singh started showing Indian films in early 1960s at the Savoy Cinema in Hayes)

1951
Amrao Bassi of 28 Albert Road who bought his house on 31 January 1951.
Fakir Singh who bought houses at 22 Inverness Road, 53-55 Hammond Road, 19 Randolph Road and 32 Avenue Road
Pritam Singh Sangha who had purchased 8 The Crescent Southall and 91 Townsend Road

1952
Karam Singh, 73 Oswald Road (from Saila Khurd)
Darshan Singh Samra of 53 Hammond Road (who later on moved to 28 Albert Road)
Harbaksh Singh, 75 Woodlands Road

1953
Mohan Singh Chatha, Gurcharan Singh Takhar and Sucha Singh Randhawa (known as 'Wadalia'), 114 Hambrough Road (who in July 1954 were joined by Gurcharan Singh)
Sarwan Singh Lalli, Chanan Singh Lalli and Pooran Singh Lalli of 55 Abbotts Road (who in 1958 moved to 47 West End Road)

1954
Jaswant Singh Dhami (founding member: IWA): 10 Dane Road
Santokh Singh Sandhu: 6 Hambrough Road (who later set up the Maharaja Restaurant on

The Broadway in partnership with Tarsem Singh Toor: IWA General Secretary)
Pritam Singh Jeer: 60 Hambrough Road (who in 1959 moved to 237 Beaconsfield Road)
Mr Harmohinder Singh Mann (an IWA Executive Committee member): 64 West End Road (who moved to 239 Beaconsfield Road)
Gurbaskh Singh Kalsi: West End Road
Brothers Jaswant Singh Bains, Davinder Singh Bains and Dyal Singh Bains, West End Road
Amar Singh Takhar (founding member:IWA) and Kartar Singh Takhar: 57 Ruskin Road
Karam Singh 'Kirti' ('Kirti' as in Freedom party): 20 Norwood Road, Southall.

1955
Bakhshish Singh Dhami, Joginder Singh Purewal and Narajan Singh along with Pritam Singh, Darshan Singh Aujla, Resham Singh, Mohan Singh (all from Isrowal village) and Tara Chand Sharma: 51 Abbotts Road
Ajit Singh Rai (founding member:IWA): 137 West End Road
Bhag Singh, Darshan Singh, Grumail Singh, Jarnail Singh, Lachman Singh, Malkit Singh, Sarwan Singh and Shanker Singh: 8 Inverness Road
Dharam Singh Sandhu and Pritam Singh Sandhu (IWA Finance Secretary:1977-1997): Lady Margaret Road.
Jaswant Singh Khalla: 118 Oswald Road

1956
Avtar Singh Bansal, Balwant Singh Grewal, Beant Singh Bassi, Hardev Singh, Malkit Singh Sohal, Rattan Singh Sora: 9 Randolph Road
Braham Dutt Jaitley, Charanjeet Singh Gill, Fateh S Bhinder, Gurpal S Dhillon, Gurdas Ram Kapur, Harbans Singh, Harcharan S Dhillon, Inder Raj Sharma, Mahinder Singh, Narinder S Dhillon, Piara Singh, Tara Singh: 23 Beaconsfield Road
Bikram Singh Sandher: 44 Avenue Road
Pritam Singh Sidhu, Sadhu Singh Sidhu, Darwara Singh Sidhu, Sarwan Singh Sidhu, Tara Singh Sidhu: 52 Saxon Road
Jagat Singh 'Jagga' (IWA EC member): 30 Abbotts Road
Harbans Singh Ruprah (founder member: IWA President): Abbotts Road

1957
Kartar Singh Sandhu: 38 Woodlands Road
Vishnu Dutt Sharma (founder member: IWA President): Beaconsfield Road
Prior to 1954 there were no recorded Panjabis listed on Ealing borough's electoral register.

By 1958 when the IWA was in its early formative stages there were an estimated 1,000 Indians, mainly men in Southall. The initial concentration of Asians was largely confined to the areas between South Road, Beaconsfield Road and the Broadway and adjacent streets.

ESTABLISHMENT OF SRI GURU SINGH SABHA SOUTHALL

By the late 1950s, the Indian community, mainly organised by a combination of individuals active in the IWA and with others more committed to or interested in maintaining their faith, began collectively meeting at Shackleton Road Hall for social, political and religious activity. This Hall was initially hired on a monthly basis to host prayers by devout Sikhs and later on prayers were extended to every Sundays on a weekly basis. In addition to the regular Sunday prayers, the Sikhs started to use this Hall on other auspicious occasions to celebrate major events such as Gurpurbs and Vaisakhi.

Given the small Indian community living in Southall at the time, there existed close relationships and linkages between those involved in the development of the Gurdwara and the IWA, with many individuals actively involved in the development of both organisations.

By 1962 the Panjabi Sikh community, actively supported by the founder members of the IWA such as Jaswant Singh Dhami, worked collectively with other more 'faith' orientated and religious Sikhs such as Surjit Singh Bilga. The IWA activists working together with local Sikhs raised funds from the community and purchased the freehold of 11 Beaconsfield Road, Southall and established the first permanent Gurdwara in Southall. This terraced house hosted regular prayers and wedding ceremonies and until today remains the property of Sri Guru Singh Sabha, Southall Gurdwara (SGSS). It continues to be used to provide accommodation for visiting priests.

In 1965 and in response to the growing Sikh community, the Gurdwara purchased an additional building, a larger hall with a small kitchen, adjacent to St. Aslems Church on The Green, Southall. This new building enabled the Gurdwara to accommodate larger congregations and for the first time provide sufficient space for wedding ceremonies.

In 1969/70, a third site, housing a milk diary was purchased on Havelock Road and became the permanent home for the SGSS Gurdwara. In the 1990s a new Gurdwara was constructed transforming this site and resulting in the development of the largest Sikh Temple in Europe.

After the relocation of the SGSS to its new Havelock Road site, the Gurdwara Hall on The Green, became unused. In 1979, some members of Southall Youth Movement (SYM), who were also associated with the SGSS's Kabaadi Club, relocated from the weight training club run from the SYM Centre at 12 Featherstone Road and took over the Gurdwara Hall on The Green, Southall. This hall began to be used by the SGSS Kabaadi Club members and others interested in wrestling and a weightlifting club cum gym was established by these volunteers.

In 2016, this old Hall on The Green is in the process of being converted by SGSS into a new modern multi- functional gymnasium and centre.

Sidney Bidwell MP addressing community meeting at Featherstone School Hall, 1976

The first *Nagar Kirtan* from The Green Gurdwara to Havelock Road Gurdwara, January 1967

EARLY INDIAN BUSINESSES IN SOUTHALL

From the late 1940s to the early 1950s many Indians travelled from Aldgate, East London and Shepherds Bush areas to work in Southall but the daily commute took a long time and the train and bus fares were high. This along with the availability of work in and around Southall area encouraged these early Panjabis to purchase and rent houses in Southall. The early Panjabi settlers in Southall state that originally one Fikar Singh (known as 'Fakiria') had a café in Aldgate East, London and along with Pritam Singh Sangha ('Bhai') and his business partner Jarnail Singh Ghuru, were some of the first Indians to move from Aldgate area to settle in Southall and establish businesses.

Pritam Singh Sangha had come to Britain in 1950 and was also a friend of 'Fakiria', initially stayed in Aldgate and along with many of his compatriots commuted daily to Southall to work at the Rubber factory and both later settled in Southall after some months.

Pritam Singh Sangha and Jarnail Singh Ghuru together opened the first Indian business, a coffee shop, named Bridge Café on 8 The Crescent Southall around 1950/51. 14 people including the family of Bhai Pritam Singh Sangha lived on top of this Café. This Café was then converted into the first Indian owned grocery shop in Southall, named *Props Sangha and Co (London) Ltd: Merchants and importers; Indian Foodstuffs.* Prior to opening this business, they had both been engaged in suppling 'door to door' groceries to Indians using a van along with other Indians, some of whom were later to start their own businesses.

The early Panjabi entrepreneurs and suppliers, responding to the lack of Indian foodstuffs within the High Street chainstores and local shops also began supplying foods to local Panjabis using mobile vans and going house to house. These included Messrs. Jaswant Singh Grewal, Bakshish Singh Bassi (known as 'Bakshi' and Bassi who later opened Panjab Stores) and Piara Singh Mann (who later opened a grocery shop on Northcote Avenue in 1962) and a Mr. Kalsi. Mr. Rattan Singh Sandhu who was involved in setting up the Indian Workers' Association was also involved in this type of work.

Mr. Bakshish Singh Bassi, known locally also as Bakshi and Bassi, is associated with opening the second Indian grocery shop in Southall. Originally he had opened a shop on Talbot Road (Old Southall) but in 1962 relocated and opened a shop (Panjab Stores) on Beaconsfield Road (between Hambrough Road and Abbotts Road). Mr Bassi had also previously been involved in working as a 'door to door' groceries' supplier.

Mr. Bassi's relative, Sohan Singh Dosanjh, subsequently opened a shop (Doaba Stores) also on Beaconsfield Road, next to Beaconsfield Junior School, which was later run by the Dosanjh family. In November 1962, Mohamad Aslam (Labour Councillor: Norwood Green Ward: 2016) bought and ran a shop on 222A Beaconsfield Road jointly with his brother-in-law which was subsequently named Sunny. At this time the Teji brothers were also running a grocery shop on 1 Beaconsfield Road, which was subsequently bought by Mohan Singh Chatha, and run as a family business for several years.

Mr. Pritam Singh Sandhu (IWA Finance Secretary: 1977-1997) was also engaged in supplying 'door to door' groceries along with supplying goods to other local Asians involved in the same trade.

Pritam Singh Sangha ('Bhai'), first Indian shop owner in Southall.

Shop of Pritam Singh Sangha, 8 The Crescent

Ajit Singh Rai (founder member and later President of IWA) along with Lashkar Singh Basra, opened the first Asian business, an Indian General Store, on 139 The Broadway, in 1962. Shortly afterwards, Ajit Singh Rai assisted Abdul Chaudhry and Mr Kailash Kohli to secure leases and open the first Restaurant and first Insurance businesses respectively in Southall on The Broadway. Mr. Abdul Chaudhry's family continues to run this family business to this day and is one of the most prominent business families with a presence on The Broadway today.

By the mid-1960s, Indian businesses began to spring up throughout Southall. Gurbachan Singh Gill opened the first Indian Office Licence liquor store on South Road and Sidhu Textiles opened one of the first clothing shop on The Broadway. Sagoo and Takhar opened the first Asian restaurant in Old Southall on The Green Southall and adjacent to the Dominion Cinema. With an increasing Asian population, with white businesses taking flight from Southall, the Asian immigrant community began to take over and set up businesses, catering for the different needs of diverse and increasing numbers of Asian consumers. Over the coming years, many other families became household names while innumerable others made their fortunes from property and in other business sectors.

The children of this first generation of immigrants either took over the running of the family businesses or went into further education to emerge as doctors, pharmacists, lawyers, accountants and professionals in their own rights, leading to the diversification in Asian businesses that we take for granted today. The myth of the Asian 'corner shop' open 7 days a week, ridiculed and joked about for years came of age, became mainstream and respectable, and their concept began to be reproduced by multi-national companies.

Fakir Singh *('Fakiria')*, one of the first Indians to purchase a house and business in Southall

The Ruprah family business on The Broadway. Messrs: Toor and Rai (3rd & 4th L), Mrs and Mr. Ruphah (7th & 8th L)

SIKHS AND RACIAL DISCRIMINATION

The vast majority of the early Panjabis were turban wearing Sikhs who on arrival or shortly thereafter were forced to contemplate the unimaginable step of cutting their hair and removing their turbans, a central part of their faith and identity. This sacrifice was enforced on them due to the additional discrimination Sikhs faced within employment, where employers would either disguise their discrimination under the pretext of health and safety laws or simply tell Sikhs to go and have their hair cut and turban removed before they could be considered for employment. This discrimination partly became internalised and fait accompli, such that by the time their families and children began to join them in the early 1960s, the practice of cutting their own children's long hair and removing their turbans was seen as a necessary step to protecting their children from racial discrimination and to helping them assimilate into the indigenous society.

Until 1965 there was no law in Britain which prohibited discrimination on racial or religious grounds and Sikhs continued to be subject to racial and religious discrimination in education, employment and other fields. Sikhs were not legally protected against discrimination under the Race Relations Acts of 1965 or the Race Relations Act of 1976, as Sikhs were not recognised as a distinct 'racial or ethnic' group under the meaning of these Acts and this anti- discriminatory legislation did not cover religious discrimination.

Within this framework, the Sikhs struggled and launched campaigns to fight against racial and religious discrimination. A number of prominent national legal cases feature in the struggle to secure equality and to end this appalling religious discrimination.

In the case of Panesar v Nestlé Co Ltd [1980], the Court of Appeal held that a rule forbidding the wearing of beards in the respondent's chocolate factory was justifiable within the meaning of section 1 (1) (b) (ii) on hygienic grounds, notwithstanding that the proportion of Sikhs who could [sc conscientiously] comply with it was considerably smaller than the proportion of non-Sikhs who could comply with it.

In July 1978, a Sikh boy, Gurinder Singh Mandla was refused entry to Park Grove School, Birmingham, because his father refused to make him stop wearing a turban and cut his hair. The school maintained that wearing a turban would be against the school uniform rules and that it would not accept Gurinder if he insisted on wearing a turban.

The case (Mandla vs Lee) was taken to the County Court and the Appeal Court and both courts ruled that Sikhs were not a racial or ethnic group. However, the House of Lords Appeal was successful and it issued a landmark ruling which determined that Sikhs were indeed a 'racial group' and set a legal precedent on the determinants of 'racial and an ethnic' groups. This case established legal history and discrimination against Sikhs became illegal under the Race Relations Act.

The campaign on the right of Sikhs to ride motor cycles without helmets, spearheaded by Baldev Singh Chahal and supported by Sikhs throughout the country was another milestone in Sikh campaigns for justice and equality.

Darshan Singh Giani (standing) with Sant Fateh Singh (2nd left) and others

IWA and CARL leaders with Sidney Bidwell MP protesting against racialist immigration laws in central London

'The local barber would refuse to cut Sikhs' hair as it was too long. In our house, I would first cut the hair of those that arrived from India and after this they would go to the Barber'.
　　Joginder Singh Saroe

'As a young Sikh boy, aged 8, my hair were sacrificed at the alter of 'assimilation'.
　　Balraj Purewal

Community members attending a funeral

Mrs. Ruprah (1st R): Mr Dhami (2nd R) welcoming a new arrival

COMMUNAL LIVING AND SUPPORT NETWORKS

During the 1950s and up to the early 1960s, Indian immigrants experienced racial discrimination in securing rented accommodation, securing mortgages and purchasing houses. This led to multiply occupation, often with 15-20 men living in a single 3 bed terraced house, with usage of beds being shared and alternated between those working day shifts and night shifts.

Preparation of meals was a shared and communal activity within all households with everyone contributing towards buying and cooking food. Cooking was organised and shared collectively within each household, with meals comprising of a basic daily diet of daal, basic English vegetables and rotis, given the scarcity of Indian vegetables. Meat dishes were reserved for special occasions and it was not until the early 1960s that meat, mostly chicken, began to feature as a dish especially on weekends.

During the 1950s and early 1960s, any new person arriving in Britain was supported and provided with free accommodation and food and it was only when they had secured paid employment that they were asked to contribute their share towards the communal food and rent costs.

The 'izatt' (respect) shown by the younger adults to older adults, to those who came from the same villages or were related directly or even indirectly emanated from a sense of duty, obligation and responsibility which had been inherited from their upbringing back in the Panjab, was quintessentially Indian. The unselfish generosity and benevolent values underpinning their commitment to their kith, kin and community are almost unimaginable commitments nowadays.

It was not until the early 1960s that the wives and children of those settled in Britain began arriving in large numbers. These new arriving families themselves settled into already overcrowded houses and it was common for 2 and sometimes 3 entire families, including numerous children of varying ages, living in a single house. Despite the overcrowding, harsh conditions and the need to adjust within a new environment, the established communal way of living remained reinforced and the bonds between different families were such that each household in effect operated as an extended family.

'The only place we could get atta (flour) was from the bakery on The Broadway. We would go there and buy a 100kg bag of flour and carry it home'.
Santokh Singh Sandhu

Mr. Dhami (standing) and friends sharing a communal meal

RACISM IN EMPLOYMENT

Under the Birth Nationality Act 1948, citizens from all Commonwealth countries had the right to live and work in Britain without any restrictions. After World War II, Britain looked for Labour from its former colonies, including the Indian sub-continent for its reconstruction efforts and to meet its labour shortages. In the 1940s and 1950s the demand for labour was prevalent in manual, low paid and dirty jobs which white workers did not want to do and due to this immigrant workers were not regarded as posing a threat to white workers.

Finding work was extremely difficult with immigrant workers subjected to overt racial discrimination, often turned away and refused employment. Racism in employment was rife and started at the factory gate where the 'Gatekeeper' would either refuse to allow 'coloured immigrants' into their factory premises or inform those making enquiries about job vacancies that no jobs were available despite the 'vacancies' signs being openly displayed in front of the factory gates. Those in employment where routinely subjected to unequal wages and harsher working conditions than their white counterparts.

The Middlese Gazettte and County Times (1 March 1958) highlighted the plight of the crisis of work shortages facing Indians citing ' many Indians who come and settle in Southall are unemployed and find difficulties in finding employment'. According to it, 60 Indians were unemployed while others estimated that the figure was much higher.

Indian workers with little or no knowledge of English were vulnerable to exploitation and victimisation of trade union activists was rife. The employment prospects of educated Indians who spoke English, possessed qualifications or had worked as professionals back home were no better and they were forced into manual jobs as the first step into employment.

Some of the main local factories at which Indians were employed included R. Woolfe's Rubber factory, Batchelor Foods, Sunblest Bakery, Mothers Pride Bakery (The Broadway, Southall), Quaker Oats (Southall), Rockware Glass Factory (Greenford) and Langley Ford.

'Everyone was a worker. Whether someone was a doctor in India, here they did Labour – then they went into their field. That was discrimination. The white person with the qualifications would get the job. They would not give the job to our Indians.

It was a question of Black and White'.
    Ajit Rai

'I would walk around all day, going from factory to factory to look for a job'.
    Om Dogra

Len Murray, General Secretary of Trade Union Congress addressing public rally to commemorate Indian Republic Day at Dominion Cinema, February 1975

Mr. Mohinder Padda, IWA General Secretary addressing a political meeting at Dominion cinema

RACISM AND TRADE UNIONS

The exploitation of the newly arriving immigrants was partly due to their lack of knowledge of workers' unions along with a lack of any historical experience or background of joining or engaging within trade unions. This exploitation was further exasperated and perpetuated by early attitudes towards immigrant workers and the racism within the trade union movement itself. In the 1950s there existed agreements, between the trade unions and the employers, to set quotas on the numbers of immigrants that would be employed in a particular factory or work section. Discrimination in the form of unequal wages and unfair treatment of immigrant and 'coloured' workers was commonplace.

During the 1950s and 1960s, the Trade Union Congress (TUC) argued that black workers did not integrate with white workers. In 1969, the TUC opposed a motion challenging immigration controls and for positive action to promote anti-discrimination legislation. The TUC failed to oppose the Commonwealth Immigrants Act 1968 and the Immigration Act 1971, which the IWA along with other national immigrant organisations and anti-racism groups across the country, vehemently opposed and campaigned against.

The national anti-immigrant context was such that Peter Grifftins, Tory Candidate in Smethwick Birmingham in the 1964 General Election, beat a Labour Minister and used the slogan *'If you want a nigger for a neighbour vote Labour'*. On 20 April 1968, Enoch Powell made his infamous anti-immigration *'Rivers of Blood'* speech attacking Commonwealth immigration and anti-discrimination legislation and stoking resentment against immigrants.

In 1969 the National Front organised a March along The Broadway in Southall under the slogan *'Send them Back'*. 200 workers from AEC (British Leyland), a local engineering firm located near the Iron Bridge (Southall) joined this March. The Union at AEC had agreed a quota with management on the number of Asian workers that could be employed within this factory.

Despite these immense hurdles, the IWA and the Trade Union Movement were to forge a close working relationship, work collaboratively and in partnership over the following decades. Len Murray, Bill Morris and other leading national trade union leaders, attended and addressed various meetings organised by IWA in Southall and collaborated and shared platforms at joint national rallies on workers' rights.

Through effective campaigning, self-help and organising unionisation amongst immigrant workers particularly in the 1960s and 1970s, the IWA emerged as one of the leading national organisations representing the interests of black workers, their rights and struggles.

An open and blatant de-facto 'colour bar' was accepted or operated in many factories with some local Trade Unions reaching agreements with employers on quotas on the number of Asian workers that they would employ in their factory.

'The discrimination was fairly institutional in those days and no one batted an eyelid at that time. So it was not surprising that the time came when they wanted to stand up for themselves'.
　　Oliver New, Chair, Ealing Trades Council

Jimmy Barzey, Afro-Caribbean community leader addressing public meeting at Dominion cinema Ballroom. (L-R): M.Padda, A.Rai and S.Bidwell MP

IWA national demonstration against immigration laws: Hyde Park, 1971

DISCRIMINATION IN HOUSING

Discrimination in housing was commonplace with single men searching for rented accommodation being told there was no accommodation available despite signs saying 'room to let' being openly displayed in front of houses. This blatant racism in housing was unashamedly public and exemplified by landlords displaying signs openly declaring *'No Coloureds'* or *'No Blacks'.*

Overcrowding and multiple occupation was commonplace until the mid-1960s with as many as 15 to 20 single men forced to live in a standard 3 bedroom terraced house. *'Hot bedding',* with beds being constantly occupied and switched between those working day and night shifts became necessary under such conditions. Glebe and Northcote wards in Southall emerged as having the worst overcrowding in the country. The initial concentration of Asians was largely confined to the area between South Road, Beaconsfield Road and The Broadway. This led to hostility from the white community which started moving out of Southall and into better housing and neighbourhoods.

White residents urged and pressed Ealing Council to use Compulsory Purchase Orders to buy vacant properties to prevent immigrants buying them. In July 1963, 140 residents of Palgrave Avenue urged Ealing Council to buy properties in the area which 'are likely to be bought by coloured people'.

In August 1963, The West Middlesex Gazette further took up this growing resentment and opposition and reported on a deputation and a petition, signed by 625 Southall residents to Ealing Council. 'Stop Immigrants Buying Houses, Residents Urge: halt the silent invasion say petitioners'.

The following week angry white residents disrupted a Council meeting with one demonstrator shouting: *'We want peace and quiet on our streets – not Indians'*

Efforts by Indians to buy houses were referred to as *'the silent invasion'.* Many of the 'problems' (of Indians overcrowding) were concentrated in the Hambrough ward and particularly at the lower end of Beaconsfield Road.

The Asians on the one hand lived in overcrowded conditions and on the other hand in housing which lacked even the very basic amenities. The majority of Asian men went to have a bath, initially at the baths situated at Southall Town Hall and later on at the public baths in Ealing Town Hall, once a week and usually on a weekend.

Simultaneously Asians experienced great difficulty in securing mortgages on one hand and on the other faced opposition from white residents when purchasing houses. White residents often objected to the sale of houses to Asians on the grounds that Asian landlords created overcrowding, feared devaluation of their own properties or that any 'influx' of Asians would create social problems in their neighbourhoods. The Southall Residents' Association, a front for the racist National Front, played on these concerns and created a climate of resentment and hostility towards Asians in Southall.

In response to this white hostility and opposition, Ealing Council tried to implement a 15-year residential qualification eligibility rule for Council housing, as part of its efforts to effectively deny Asians from even applying for Council housing, until they had lived in the borough for 15 years. This 15-year ruling was later outlawed under the first Race Relations Act of 1965, which became effective on 25th October 1968. This Act prohibited discrimination in housing and employment on the basis of race, nationality and ethnicity.

The price of an average 3 bedroom terraced house circa 1955 ranged from £1,600 to £2,000 and the average salary of workers was between £7 to £14 per week with overtime.

These early settlers broke the overt discrimination and barriers in housing through supporting one and another to purchase freehold properties which then accommodated more of their kith and kin and others who were arriving from their villages.

To Let

Furnished flat, Lounge, double bedroom, single bedroom, dining room, kitchen, bathroom, box room.

Quiet couple. No children, animals or coloured peoples.

Telephone: Ealing 8167 (evening)
    Advertisement in Middlesex Gazette and County Times: 25 October 1958

'That time in housing – white people would not sell us houses. They were saying 'No for Indians - No for Blacks'. This was a type of insult which also is hurtful'.
    Surjit Singh Bilga: former IWA EC member and founder/Trustee: Sri Guru Singh Sabha Southall

'We used to have some pubs in Southall. They would not serve you beer. Sometimes they would just say 'get out' because at that time there was no anti-discrimination law. But the others would let you come in, but you had to wait your turn after he had served the local people, even though they have come after you.'.
    Dr. Sathi Ludhianvi

SOCIAL AND CULTURAL LIFE IN THE 1950s AND 60s

Working long unsocial hours, the main priority amongst the early immigrants was to save money to send back home to their families and to purchase their own houses in this country. These immigrants did not frequent local pubs, an established practice amongst their local English working class counterparts, as it was not part of their 'cultural way of life' and given the potential threat of physical attacks and racial abuse that those who did venture out were often subjected to.

Many early immigrants had to adjust to a totally different way of living, including coming to terms with a different social etiquette. Many of the 'educated' immigrants would teach their countrymen the social manners to be followed, such as waiting in a queue for a bus and not jumping the queue, allowing women to go first, not spitting on the street and other basic etiquettes which the English were perceived to adhere to and value.

In the early 1950s, the main community activity was centered around the Sinclair Road Gurdwara, which after prayers on Sundays doubled up and acted as a social centre where Panjabis could come together, socialise in and get news about their families, villages and country.

By 1957, the IWA became organising social activity at Southall Community Centre, Bridge Road on Sundays enabling local Indians to come together socially, access Indian newspapers, play cards and celebrate key events such as Indian Independence Day, Vaisakhi and Diwali. On 17 August 1957, IWA organised its first public event at Southall Community Centre to celebrate the 11th Independence Day of India and approximately 500 people attended. A representative of Indian High Commission and Darbara Singh (Chief Minister of Panjab) along with local dignitaries also attended and spoke at this gathering.

The local Panjabis also hosted social political and religious meetings and activity at Shackleton Hall, Shackleton Road, Southall which they hired on Sundays and for special events.

With the arrival of families in the early 1960s, family outings to Southall Park on Sundays became a regular social and recreational pastime. By the late 1960s, groups of Asian elders began to congregate in the local parks to socialise and play cards, their favourite pastime, much to the annoyance and resentment of local Park Attendants, many of whom actively discouraged these gatherings by forcibly dispersing Asian elders away from their parks.

Wrestling was traditionally the most popular sport amongst Indians. However as many did not possess televisions, it was a common sight in the mid-1960s to see large groups of Indian men gathered outside the TV shops on The Broadway and on South Road, watching wrestling matches every Saturdays between 3pm to 4pm.

The first Bhangra team was set up in 1963 in Featherstone Road High School by the first batch of young Indians entering High Schools. The demand and popularity from across the country led this Bhangra group, called The Great Indian Dancers, to perform nationally and in due course it started charging for its performances. The Great Indian Dancers established themselves as the best Bhangra group in the country and received many accolades, nationally and internationally. In 1965, the IWA itself set up its own Bhangra group and offered free performances across the country particularly at cultural and political events organised by Indian organisations.

The first Indian films were shown by the IWA at Southall Community Centre and later on

IWA social event. (L-R): Yadvinder Singh, Virendra Sharma, Vishnu Sharma, Mr. Kartar Takhar

the IWA started renting the Dominion Cinema in Southall. At the same time other Indian entrepreneurs also started showing Indian films in a rented cinema, Essolodo, which was part of the 'Savoy' chain of cinemas and located on 466 Uxbridge Road, Hayes near The Grapes junction.

The purchase of Dominion Cinema by IWA in December 1965 marked a turning point in the social life of Asians who flocked with their families to watch Indian films particularly on Sundays. The Dominion Cinema became the main, if not the only, 'community hub' for all social cultural and political activity in Southall, including IWA's Indian Independence Day celebrations, wrestling contests, new film releases and political meetings.

In the early 1960s weddings were miniscule affairs often consisting of a small 'barat' (wedding party) of 5 to 10 men in attendance and on occasions being entertained in a house. After 1965 weddings slowly began to be scaled up with the opening of the Gurdwara on The Green and access to the Dominion Cinema's ballroom area which started the trend for larger 'wedding functions', accommodating 100 or so guests.

On 10 October 1965, the BBC broadcast its first programme for Hindi and Urdu speaking viewers called *'In Logon Se Miliye'* (Let me Introduce You to These People), which in 1966 was replaced by *'Apne He Ghar Samajhiya'* (Make Yourself at Home) which in 1968 became *'Nai Zindagi Nay Jeeva'* (New Way New Life) every Sunday mornings. This one hour programme starting at 9am became essential viewing and featured an English class to teach and introduce Asians to the British way of life, news, advice on immigration and a cultural performance from renowned Asian artists. Vishnu Sharma, IWA President, featured regularly in the slot dedicated to providing advice on immigration matters to viewers.

Balbir Singh Purewal, Health Minister, Panjab addressing IWA meeting at Dominion cinema

Great Indian Dancers (Southall) Bhangra Group performing

IWA leaders with Swaran Singh, Indian Foreign Minister and Umrao Singh, Panjab Minister (R: 4th & 6th) and other delegates

Deputy Prime Minister of India, Jagjivan Ram attending IWA function

Community members attending IWA public meeting in Dominion cinema

IWA public meeting with guest speaker Chaudhary Darshan Singh, Congress MLA (seated 1st left)

Function in honour of Prime Minister Indira Gandhi's visit to London

IWA members with Indian central Government Minister

IWA members and supporters in front of The Maharaja Restaurant on The Broadway owned by Mr. Tarsem Toor & Mr. Santokh Sandhu on The Broadway

Darshan Singh Giani with Douglas Hume, UK Government Minister

SPORTS

From the mid-1960s to mid-1970s, the Asian youth population increased substantially and with this emerged a slow but gradual interest and participation in sport activities.

The first Asian football team was established by Kesar Singh Bhatti in 1968. Kesar Bhatti was himself a *'Panjab Select',* an Indian footballer who had played at State level for Panjab and competed at national Inter-State football tournaments. His interest in and commitment to football motivated him to approach and influence a reluctant IWA leadership to support him in his efforts to establish an Asian football team in Southall.

Kesar Bhatti started training local Asian young people at Southall Park and established the first football team in Southall which initially played under the name of IWA Southall. Despite the absence of changing facilities, a marked pitch and goal posts, his team of enthusiastic players would assemble most evenings after school and at weekends at Southall Park, whatever the weather conditions. Within a year, players of this team became well known amongst local young people and the team's practice sessions attracted many younger and aspiring footballers. The football team entered the Asian sports tournaments organised and sponsored annually by the bigger and well established Gurdwaras in towns such as Coventry, Gravesend, Birmingham and in later years in Leicester, Southall, Derby and other towns. These annual Asian tournaments also featured Kabaadi, wrestling, hockey as well as track and field events.

Kesar Bhatti's first football team played under the name of IWA for a short period and then under the name of 'Jolly Brothers'. Later on this IWA (Southall) Football team secured sponsorship from Sri Guru Singh Sabha Gurdwara, entered the local Middlesex League and played under the name of Singh Sabha Southall and became a highly successful team, winning numerous Asian tournaments as well as league titles.

This Football team laid the foundation for promoting the sport amongst the seconder generation of Asians, giving them the confidence and inspiring many to emulate their seniors. By 1970, the interest in football generated by this team led to the establishment of the Indian Youth Club and Yadvindra football teams in Southall. Like their seniors these aspiring young Asians also entered into local leagues and played in national Asian tournaments.

As part of its work to meet the needs of the increasing and younger Asian community and to promote sports, the IWA also set up a VolleyBall team.

Southall Football Team, 1969: Kesar Singh Bhatti (Manager) Back Row, 3rd from left

IWA Volley Ball Team, 1975

SECTION 2

This section provides information on the founding of the Indian Workers' Association (Southall).

THE IWAs IN BRITAIN IN THE 1900s: Fighting for Indian Independence

Bharti Mazdoor Sabhas (Indian Workers' Associations) had existed in Britain for many decades before IWA Southall was established. These IWAs were established to raise consciousness of the struggle for Indian Independence in Britain and to protect and promote the welfare of working class Indians in Britain. The first IWA in Britain was set up in Coventry in 1938 and later on other IWAs were set up in Birmingham, Manchester, Newcastle, Wolverhampton, Sheffield, Glasgow, London and Bradford.

Shaheed Udham Singh became associated with the IWA movement when he came to England to avenge the murder of his father and the Indians who were massacred by General Reginald Dyer at Jallianwala Bagh in Amritsar on 13 April 1919. Under the command of General Dyer, British Indian Army troops had open fired on civilians who had assembled to participate in the annual Baisakhi celebrations in Amritsar. The brutality of Dyer's crime was evidenced by the fact that he continued firing at the civilians for about ten minutes, until the ammunition supply was almost exhausted. The British Government released figures stating that 379 civilians had been killed and 1,200 wounded. The Indian National Congress at the time estimated that nearly 1,000 civilians had been killed.

Shaheed Udham Singh also visited and stayed at the Gurdwara on Sinclair Road, Shepherds Bush, London and subsequently shot General Dyer at Caxton Hall, London. Shaheed Udham Singh was hanged for killing General Dyer.

After Independence of India on 15 August 1947, the work of these IWAs went into decline.

However, the IWAs were revived in the 1950s by the new generation of immigrants from India, many of whom had been involved in the freedom struggle, had links and affiliations to the Gadhar Party and the Community Party in India. This new generation of immigrants built upon the name and organisational structure which had been created by their predecessors and which had existed for decades as the seeds for developing the new Bharti Mazdoor Sabhas (Indian Workers' Associations) to address the new needs and challenges facings Indian workers in Britain. These new IWAs were equally committed to maintaining links with their motherland and to promoting equality in India.

Bharti Mazdoor Sabha (IWA) branches began to be reactivated and established throughout Britain and the IWA Coventry branch was one of the first to be reactivated. IWA branches were set up in Wolverhampton and Southall in 1956 and in Birmingham in 1959.

Given the emergence of IWAs in different cities, the need for a centralisation of the IWAs was identified and promulgated and in 1959, IWA Great Britain (GB) emerged as the national representative body comprising of a federation of local IWA branches. The key proponents within these new localised IWA branches as well as the leadership of IWA (GB) were predominately socialists and individuals aligned with the politics of the Communist Party of India (CPI).

Some of the founding activists of the IWA (Southall), although themselves aligned to or with CPI affiliations, chose not to be part of the IWA (GB) federation structure. The IWA (Southall) leadership did not want to be dominated by communists or be specifically aligned to the CPI but wanted IWA (Southall) to remain a secular and non-sectarian organisation, evolving into a mass

Jaswant S. Dhami, Amar S. Takhar, Ajit S. Rai, Jagat Ram, Vishnu D. Sharma and other IWA EC members in meeting at Southall Community Centre, 1958

Surjt Singh Bilga (R: 8th) and Jaswant Singh Dhami (R: 9th) welcoming striking workers' delegate from Glasgow

movement to bring together Indians of all political persuasions. Consequently, IWA (Southall) became a separate independent body and not a part of the IWA (GB) structure.

From these early years to the mid-1960s, while both the IWAs co-operated on matters of mutual interest and concern, a schism between the two IWAs developed and widened due to differences on political thinking and strategies on issues such as race relations and inequalities facing Indian workers in Britain and in India. IWA (Southall) was perceived to be a more assimilative body, wishing to engage with state bodies and with a greater emphasis on educating and integrating Indians into British society whilst IWA (GB) wanted to change institutions through challenging state racism and opposed engagement with governmental bodies that it felt perpetuated racism and inequality.

IWA (Southall) along with the other IWA (GB) branches began to organise workers and address the new challenges facing the increasing number of new immigrants, the majority of whom could not read, write or speak English, were confined to manual and labouring jobs, subject to unscrupulous and exploitative employers and racial discrimination.

IWA leaders and members including Messrs: Rai, Dhillon, Ram, Brar, Dhami, Sharma and Ruprah meeting UK Government Officials

FORMATION OF IWA SOUTHALL: 1956

Many of the founding members of IWA Southall were aligned to the Communist Party of India, had been involved in the freedom struggle, engaged in or interested in Indian politics but above all had an undiminishable commitment to serve their community and to help alleviate the problems their countrymen faced in Britain.

The IWA's association and alignment with socialist values and socialism became embedded into and was reflected by its formal organisational structure. It was governed by an Executive Committee, a hierarchal leadership structure comprising of President; Vice President; General Secretary; Deputy Secretary; Office Secretary; Finance Secretary; Cultural Secretary; Education Secretary; Propaganda Secretary; Welfare Secretary and Sports Secretary and 11 Executive Committee members. At one stage it established a post of Secretary Without Portfolio within its Executive Committee, in response to and illustrative of the demands amongst members to hold titles.

The founder members of IWA included Amar Singh Takhar, Jaswant Singh Dhami, Ajit Singh Rai, Harbans Singh Ruprah, Rattan Singh Sandhu and Vishnu Dutt Sharma who set up an 'embryonic' group which drove the development of the organisation, holding meetings at different houses.

Rattan Singh Sandhu became linked to the IWA which later emerged as IWA (GB) and was one of the first people involved in driving the establishment of an IWA in Southall. However during the early months of the formation of IWA (Southall), there was a divergence between the approach of Rattan Singh Sandhu, who desired an IWA which was more aligned to or part of the wider emerging IWA (GB) movement in Britain at that time, and other local activists who saw a more independent and inclusive IWA in Southall.

From its inception and formation IWA Southall decided and committed itself to engaging a wider community and worker base and not adopt a restrictive organisational structure which would consist of or be dominated by a small centralised organising committee of a few 'elite activists'. Its founding members aspired to promote mass community and worker participation cemented by a commitment to secular values. This visionary aspiration and commitment by the founding members was to become IWA Southall's most distinguishable hallmark as it set in motion a unique and unparalleled situation within IWA Southall, unlike any other IWA in Britain, where individuals of differing political affiliations, persuasions and interests would become engaged in its membership and leadership. Hard core communists, socialists, liberals, conservatives, business people and ordinary workers actively became members, forged political alliances and engaged within IWA's work and leadership.

Whilst no exact date can be determined as to the 'official' date of establishment, there is no doubt that IWA (Southall) was established in 1956. Evidence from some of the original members confirms that IWA (Southall) was established in 1956 and that by late 1956 it had recruited an estimated 100 -200 members.

The membership fee for joining the IWA in 1956 was 2 shillings and 6 pence.

IWA delegation in meeting with Indian Government Official

Messsr Dhami and Sharma (L: 1st & 2nd) attending IWA social function

By 1957, IWA Southall was effectively operating, offering information advice and welfare support to local workers and holding activities every weekends at Southall Community Centre on Bridge Road. These activities included discussions on topical issues, English Language classes, provision of Indian newspapers as well as providing a general social and meeting point.

The first formal inaugural meetings of IWA was held in Southall on 23 March 1957 and Amar Singh Takhar, Jaswant Singh Dhami, Rattan Singh Sandhu, Vishnu Dutt Sharma, Ajit Singh Rai and Harbans Singh Ruprah were amongst those present in this meeting.

The first Annual Conference where the IWA members formally elected its first Executive Committee (EC) was held on 1 March 1958 at Southall Community Centre. At this time the IWA had around 400 members and the following Executive Committee Officers were formally elected:

President:	Amar Singh Takhar
Vice-President:	Jaswant Singh Dhami
General Secretary:	Ajit Singh Rai
Deputy Secretary:	S.S. Sandhu
Office Secretary:	K. Lal
Financial Secretary:	S.S. Gosal
Cultural Secretary:	Gurdial Singh
Education Secretary:	Rajinder Singh
Propaganda Secretary:	Gurdial Singh Bara
Welfare Secretary:	K.S. Rai
Sports Secretary:	Jaswant Singh Khan

Amar Singh Takhar, the first President of IWA, departed from Britain and returned back to his homeland to settle permanently in October 1958 and was preceded by Jaswant Singh Dhami as President of IWA.

'We would go house to house and it would take us 2 to 3 days to convince people and recruit them as members as there was no previous history of our people engaging in organisations'.
    Ajit Rai: founder member.

'In late 1956, Harbans Ruprah came to our house to recruit me and my father as IWA members. My father was not interested but I followed Mr. Ruprah outside and gave him 2 Shillings and 6 pence to become a member as I believed in self organisation and unions. I was 19 at the time'.
    Pritam Singh Sandhu: IWA Finance Secretary 1977-1997.

IWA leaders in meeting at Southall Community Centre

IWA AND SECULARISM

Secularism was enshrined and embedded into the aims, objectives and structures of the IWAs from their very inception and commitment to secular values remained central to the founders of IWA Southall.

Sikhs, Hindus, Muslims, atheists, people from different castes, people with widely differing political views, political alignments and allegiances ranging from communists, socialists, people aligned to Congress party, Akali Dal party along with business people came together under the auspices of the IWA and collectively worked to address issues facing Indians and other immigrant workers from Commonwealth countries.

A truly secular organisation: Sikhs Hindus, Muslims, Christians – Labour, Conservative, Liberal, Communists, Akalis, Congress, Atheists and others came together under the auspices of the IWA.

IWA protesting against racist immigration laws in central London: Tara Dyal and Gurpal Gill holding the IWA flag

IWA AIMS AND OBJECTS

'The Association is established for the purpose of providing for its members the means of social intercourse, mutual helpfulness, mental and moral improvement and rational recreation'

Throughout its history, the IWA, though a membership body, did not ever distinguish between members and non- members and its services were accessible and available to everyone. It supported people from all the different communities and from across the country.

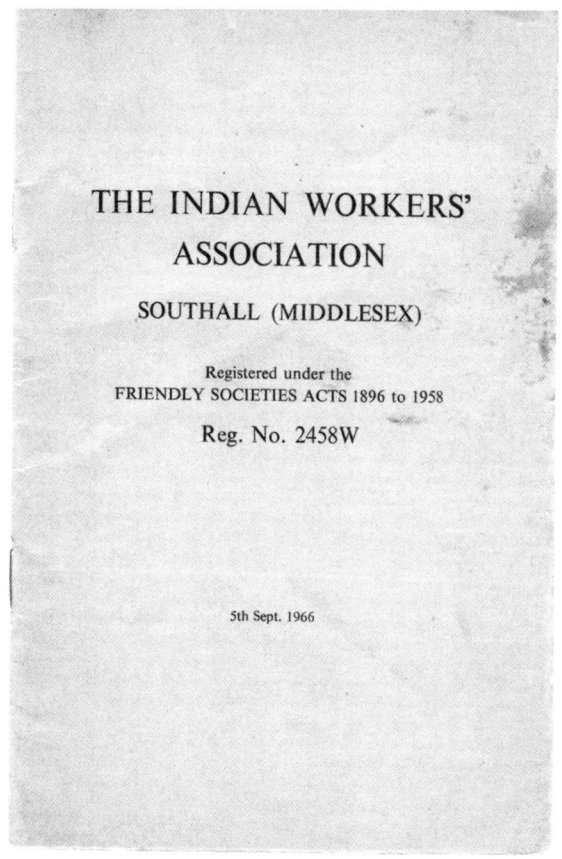

MEMBERSHIP CARD

INDIAN WORKERS' ASSOCIATION

18 Featherstone Road,
SOUTHALL, Middx. UB2 5AA. (U.K.)
(Tel: 01-574 7283)

Reg. No.................... Membership No........................

This is to acknowledge that

MR/MRS/MISS ....

of ....

is an honourable member of this Association for the year

19............ 19............

Date... *General Secretary.*

INDIAN WORKERS' ASSOCIATION
(Registered under the Friendly Societies Act).

IMPORTANT INSTRUCTIONS

Every member is requested to keep this CARD in safe custody and produce it on demand either at the gates while seeking admission for attending the Gen. Meeting of the Association or at the booking office of the Dominion Cinema Hall, The Green, Southall, Middx., while making a demand for a Concessional Ticket for cinema show.

NOTE: Please bring your membership card and medical card with you at the time of voting for I.W.A. election.

DOMINION CINEMA: Tel. no. 01-574 1681.

Usual signature
of the Card-holder...

SECTION 3

This section outlines the key areas of the work and campaigns of the IWA.

INDIANS AND IRREGULAR IMMIGRATION STATUS

In the mid-1950s, the Indian Government under Prime Minister Jawarlal Nehru, in its efforts to curb emigration into Britain, began making it extremely difficult for Indians, particularly those from rural backgrounds and Panjabis to acquire visas and passports in order to come to Britain. However similar controls were not imposed on those seeking entry as students, business people or on ex-servicemen.

Many rural Panjabis overcame this obstacle by using a combination of 'agents' to secure forged documentation and passports or visiting and using other countries as a means of entering Britain. Inevitably this led to many Panjabis living in Britain at that time not having valid passports which led to a situation whereby those with forged documents and passports could not have their Indian passports renewed or visit India. More critically it also created a situation whereby the immigration status of these Indian immigrants in Britain became 'irregular' and consequently these Indian workers were subjected to exploitation and they often lived in fear of being reported to the authorities or losing their jobs. This issue was undoubtedly one of the most pressing issues facing the early immigrants.

The IWAs worked both to help individuals facing this problem and mounted a sustained campaign to lobby the Indian High Commission to issue Indians trapped in this situation with valid Indian passports in order to prevent their exploitation and to enable them to visit or return to their homeland.

The IWA also met Prime Minister Jawarlal Nehru when he visited Britain in 1957 to discuss this and other issues facing Indians in Britain. The IWA's campaign led to the Indian High Commission in London recognising this problem and issuing new Indian Passports to those who had entered Britain using false documentation.

This was one of the first successful campaign of the IWA and it brought recognition and prestige to the IWA.

This issue of 'irregular' status persisted throughout the 1960s and 1970s and IWA continued to campaign in support of those affected and later on the IWA began its campaigns to press the British Government to grant an Amnesty for illegal immigrants from the New Commonwealth and Pakistan.

EARLY IMMIGRANTS AND TAX CLAIMS

The second major issue facing many Indian immigrants in the 1950s and 1960s and to absorb the IWA was in the area of income tax and with the tax authorities. In order to gain advantage of British personal income tax 'concessions', many Indians had made or were 'advised' to make declarations of having children when in reality they either had any children at all or had less children than their tax records showed. This enabled them to make claims for dependent children which in some cases did not exist. At the time, people could make claims for dependent children, irrespective of the fact whether those children resided with them or not.

As the tax authorities began to discover wrongful submissions and claims, it inevitably took action, launching investigations and prosecuting those found to have made or gained from wrongful claims. Those prosecuted and found guilty were sometimes subject to imprisonment. This created fear and panic and many sought advice, support and refuge from the IWA to resolve their problem.

IWA successfully negotiated with the relevant UK authorities arrangements whereby Indians were able to make the correct declarations, make outstanding repayments to recompense the tax authorities for any personal gains made, without fear of prosecution and avoid imprisonment.

Such was the scale of this problem that the IWA negotiated a deal with Board of Inland Revenue (currently HMRC) in the form of an undertaking that persons who had previously made false claims would not be prosecuted if they came forward through the IWA and voluntarily confessed.

Until as late as 1975, the IWA was helping hundreds of people with their outstanding income tax related problems.

'The IWA helped hundreds of people, who had falsely claimed for children they did not have, to sort their problems with the tax authorities and avoid being prosecuted'.
Harjinder Dhillion: former General Secretary

STRIKE AT ROCKWARE GLASS: GREENFORD

The strike at Rockware Glass is considered to be one of the first known industrial action taken by Asian workers in and around Southall at the end of 1962.

The origin of the strike is attributed to the persistent exploitation and the lack of any actions by the employers on the grievances of the Asian workforce. One of the main grievances centred on the amount of work Asian workers were forced to do and the management's failure to recruit additional staff to cover staffing shortages which were putting existing staff under enormous work pressures. These staff shortages were further accentuated by the refusal of white workers to do overtime or work weekends. It became common practice for management to force a team of 3 workers to do the work of 4 workers, creating harsh and unsafe working conditions along with resentment within the workforce. It was not uncommon for some Asian workers to be forced to work 70 hours a week.

The workforce in one section was organised around 3 shifts each manned by a 'crew' consisting of around 30 workers and production carried out 24 hours a day.

Some of the Asian workers, including Vishnu Dutt Sharma, who were active on the shop floor and worked at the factory had begun to organise and unionise the Asian workforce and to press for basic rights and fair treatment. Vishnu Sharma, who worked the night shift, finally led the grievances and staged a 'walk out' with the 'A' crew, the night crew in protest at the staffing shortages and extent of the exploitation. Crew 'B' the early morning crew, on arrival at work also walked out in sympathy and support and the strike began. By the end of their industrial action, an estimated 165 workers were sacked including Vishnu Sharma, and many left and found employment elsewhere.

The Rockware Glass strike was a seminal milestone in the history of Asian workers in their struggles for basic rights and equality and of the movement that would emerge amongst Asian workers to organise and unionise themselves, oppose exploitation and assert their rights in employment.

'I walked out on strike in solidarity with Crew A, the night shift led by Vishnu Sharma. Teams of 3 workers were forced to do the work of 4 workers regularly'.
   Bakhsish Singh Dhami.: Rockware glass factory worker: 1963

Indian women working in a sweet factory in Southall, 1976

DURA TUBE & WIRE LTD STRIKE

The Dura Tube and Wire factory in Feltham produced telephone cables and employed around 150 workers, mainly Asian. The Hungarian owner of the factory was reputed to have links with the Hungarian royalty and was referred to by the Asian workforce as 'Prince Charles' and had an anti-union reputation, vehemently opposing and thwarting any efforts to organise a union in his factory.

The issue of low wages had been consistently raised by the Asian workforce but was repeatedly rejected by the management.

The management, as part of a cost cutting exercise, closed the factory canteen which was open to workers on the night and day shifts and instead installed vending machines for staff to purchase tea, coffee and soft drinks. The workers objected to the closure of their staff canteen and also did not like the vending machine. Simultaneous they demanded that management address their ongoing grievances around low pay and their right to unionise themselves. The management's outright dismissal of the workers' grievances led to the workers organising themselves, joining a union and going on strike. The workers, led by a number of activists, including Gurdial Singh Dhami (later president of IWA: 2007-2015) and Darshan Singh Giani (later IWA President:1968-72) organised and recruited most of the workers in the factory as members of the TGWU union and went on strike for 2 weeks.

Gurdial Singh Dhami became the official shop steward and represented the workers' interests in negotiations with the management.

The IWA supported the strike actively, through giving access to the striking workers to hold meetings at its premises on 18 Featherstone Road, organising food to be delivered to the strikers who were picketing the factory, mobilising public support within the local community and helping coordinate action with the trade union.

Resham Samra and Ajit Rai of IWA supporting striking Hillingdon Hospital workers, 1996

THE R. WOOLFE'S RUBBER FACTORY

The R. Wolfe's Rubber Factory is synonymous with the early settlers from the Panjab area and occupies a unique place in their history and that of Southall's Asian community.

One of its General Managers, Mr Dunn, had served in the British Army in India with Indian Sikh soldiers and held the Sikh community in high regard, as being hard working, loyal and dedicated people. Through this relationship the early Sikhs who had served in the British Army became to go to and become employed at this factory. Word had spread about the factory within the Panjabi community and virtually all new arrivals would start employment at this factory. There are innumerable cases where a new arrival would land and come to Southall in the morning and by the afternoon would be working at this factory.

This factory was located on the main Uxbridge Road just over the Bridge on the border of Southall and Hayes. Working conditions were harsh, with Indian workers employed in jobs that their white counterparts were reluctant to do. Management, supervisory and jobs deemed 'easier or clean' remained the exclusive reserve of the white workforce with Indians confined to hard labouring and 'piece work' jobs; whilst receiving less wages than their white colleagues for similar jobs. Most of the Panjabi workers had come for villages, were not educated or literate in English and were unable to communicate their grievances in any organised manner. Individual grievances often resulted in workers being 'sacked'.

It was not until 1964 that the right to join a union was finally recognised in the factory. Despite this recognition, anti- union practices by management continued provoking a number of unofficial 'walkouts'. Unfortunately immigrant workers were reluctant to join the union as unions were primarily associated with representing the interests of white workers and the Union itself faced barriers or made little effort to seriously recruit or fight for the interests of immigrant workers.

As the Asian workforce increased, the exploitation of immigrant workers became increasing evident and blatant, fuelling demands for basic rights such as tea breaks, pay rises, ban on compulsory overtime and safer working conditions. Asian workers began to organise themselves, make collective demands and staged a number of 'walk outs' and protests. Most of the founding members of IWA or its subsequent leaders, including Ajit Singh Rai, Vishnu Dutt Sharma, Jaswant Singh Dhami, Harbans Singh Ruprah and Piara Singh Khabra had worked or were working at the Rubber factory.

With a potential strike looming, the key organisers with the active support of IWA launched a massive concerted secret and successful campaign to unionise Asian workers, recruiting an estimated 452 Indian workers as members of Transport and General Workers' Union (TGWU) in a relatively short period of time.

In November 1965, Asian workers went on strike. This strike was triggered when shop steward, Mukhtiar Singh, was suspended for reporting pilfering on the part of a chargehand to security guards. The management in turn tried to suspend Mukhtiar Singh for superfluous charges including being 10 minutes late.

600 Asian workers went on strike demanding safer working conditions and this strike lasted for seven weeks. Despite Asian workers becoming members of the TGWU, the strike was not

The R. Woolfe's Rubber factory, Uxbridge Road, Hayes on the border of Southall/Hayes

immediately declared official by the TGWU. Indian workers were not initially paid 'strike pay' which union members were entitled to receive from their Unions during period of industrial disputes and strikes. Even worse was the fact that TGWU made no move to have goods produced at Woolfe's Rubber factory boycotted by their members and workers at Ford or Vauxhall until the last week of the strike. There were some 13,000 TGWU members at Ford, and a boycott, could have made a major impact, making the strike more successful and Indian workers feel more supported.

To break the strike, the factory management deliberately tried to recruit and bring Pakistani workers from Bradford and northern towns, play on national sentiments and divide the Indian and Pakistani workers and community. The management strategy failed and it was unable to create division between the two communities.

During this strike the community rallied in support of the striking Asian workers. Pritam Singh Sangha (known as 'Bhai' - an affectionate term for older brother) owned the only Indian grocery and foodstuff shop in Southall at that time. Pritam Singh Sangha voluntarily undertook to supply free foodstuff to all striking workers and their families, who had no other source of income, so that they would not be starved back into submission and work. The IWA rallied the community in support of the strikers, raising funds and coordinating and mobilising support for the strikers.

This strike was a seminal moment in the history of the Asian community in Southall. Asian workers became to organise, join unions in increasing numbers and become active in the trade union movement as shop stewards to address discrimination both within the trade union movement as well as amongst employers. These activists, nurtured and supported by the IWA, kick started a new drive to work and campaign tirelessly to protect the interests and rights of immigrant workers and make the trade union movement both responsive and accountable to the needs of immigrant workers over the next 2 decades.

This strike was to have a devastating impact on the Asian community given the Asian workers' reliance and dependency on this factory for employment. The closure of the Rubber factory severed the umbilical cord between that factory and the Panjabi community, forcing them to seek employment in areas outside Southall in firms such as United Biscuits (Brentford), J. Lyons (Greenford), Langley Ford, AEC (British Leyland: Southall) Champion Spark Plugs (Feltham), Mother's Pride and Sunblest Bakeries, Heathrow Airport, Grunding and others.

National demonstration against immigration controls: central London, 1975

DISPERSAL AND BUSSING OF ASIAN SCHOOLCHILDREN IN SOUTHALL

During the early 1960s, an increasing number of Asian families, including children, began to arrive and settle in Southall. This new influx and increasing immigration from the Indian sub-continent led to wide spread concerns, resentment and opposition from the local indigenous white community on the adverse impact of this immigration on public services particularly in schools, housing and employment and on wider community relations.

In response to this the Government enacted and introduced a number of measures to curb and deal with the 'immigration' issue including:
- the Immigration Act 1962 to control immigration particularly from the Indian sub-continent;
- Section 11 of the Local Government Act 1966, which referred to 'substantial numbers from the Commonwealth whose language and customs differ from those of the community' and which was to provide financial support to those local authorities with substantial Commonwealth immigrant populations and to help them deal with the 'problem';
- Bussing and dispersal of 'coloured' children in education.

The national policy of dispersal and bussing of 'coloured children' was introduced in Southall in June 1965. The Government's policy stated that where there were more than 33% of immigrant children in any one class, dispersal and bussing should be introduced. Underpinning this racist policy of dispersal of coloured children was the distorted view that it was an important part of enabling the 'coloured community' to integrate into society. Even more disturbingly this policy incorporated the thinking that the presence of large numbers of 'coloured and immigrant children' in any one class undermined the education of white schoolchildren.

Asian and Afro Caribbean children were 'bussed' from Southall to other schools across the Ealing borough catchment area. A convoy of coaches descended on Southall on a daily basis and Asian mothers had to take their children to designated pick up points early in the morning and then pick them up after school. For many children this would involve getting up very early at 6:30am in order to get to the pick-up points, often returning home as late as 5:00pm. The daily route for the convoy of coaches included pick up points at Featherstone Road School and Oswald Road (back of Beaconsfield Road School). Many children would be found asleep when the coaches returned to their base, due to children having missed their drop off points due to sheer exhaustion arising from the long daily journeys.

The biggest pick up point was at Featherstone Avenue where by 1975, 600 children and their parents would congregate at the school every morning to be picked up by a convoy of buses. Dispersed children were bussed to schools between 2 and 7 miles away from Southall. Ealing Council owned 6 radio-controlled coaches and used, on contract from private companies, 58 buses along with 6 mini-buses. The 53 seater coaches took up to 73 children.

The IWA campaigned vigorously against the introduction of bussing and the racism underpinning this policy, arguing that the solution was to build more schools in Southall. Southall had 3 primary schools, Beaconsfield Road, Tudor Road and Featherstone. There was however a

Mr. Gurdial Dhami's children, Kamaljit, Harminder and Daljit, waiting to be bussed, Oswald Road, 1974

small minority within the Asian community who felt that bussing was beneficial in 'integrating' Asian children into the host community.

In January 1975, '2,989 children of primary age were bussed and a further 1,800 of secondary school age made their own way to secondary schools from Southall.

A decade long campaign spearheaded by the IWA finally led to the ending of bussing in 1976.

Though 'bussing' was declared illegal in 1976, the practice continued until about 1981. Between 1976 and 1981 the justification for continuing this racist practice was no longer on grounds of integration but on the grounds that there was lack of funding to build new schools in Southall.

The racist policy of 'Bussing' of black school children was based on the distorted notion that the presence of large numbers of 'coloured and immigrant children' undermined the education of white schoolchildren.

From 1965 to mid 1970s thousands of immigrant children were bussed out of Southall. Not a single white child was bussed into Southall.

Jaswinder Singh Sidhu went on hunger strike in protest against the bussing of his son, Rajan, aged 5, in 1976.

Protest against Ealing Council's discriminatory policy of 'Bussing' of Asian schoolchildren

DOMINION CINEMA: THE GOLDEN YEARS

The Dominion Cinema was the largest cinema in London. It was a grand building with a huge entrance area where cinema-goers could congregate and purchase tickets, with a ticket booth situated in the centre of this area and which could accommodate more than 300 people. Two large entrances flowed from this open ticketing area and into the ground floor of the cinema auditorium which had a capacity for 1,200 seats. In between these entrances were two separate flights of stairs leading to the Ballroom and to the first floor cinema gallery which had a capacity of a further 600 seats. The ground floor and gallery areas had a combined capacity of 1,856 seats. At the front of the cinema screen was a large stage for performances and in front of this stage was situated a boxing and wrestling ring. The Ballroom could accommodate around 300 people and became the first real venue for Indian wedding parties in Southall.

The IWA initially hired the Dominion Cinema from around 1959-1960 and began showing Indian films on Sundays. This proved extremely popular, attracting huge crowds in the absence of any other social outlet or activity for Asians at the time and by 1964 the IWA was considering its acquisition on a permanent basis.

The popularity of films was such that 'House Full' sign became a common sight and people queued in their hundreds to purchase tickets. Going to the Dominion Cinema to watch an Indian movie became a feature and almost a way of life for most Asian families on weekends. During Intermission breaks, hundreds of cinema-goers would flock from the Cinema's auditorium halls and into its large foyer area to eat samosas and 'sholay bhuturay'.

The IWA awarded the first catering contract to serve Asian food to cinema-goers at Dominion Cinema to Mr. Abdul Majid Chauhdry and later on in around 1964 to Messrs. Sagoo and Takhar. Both Mr. Chaudhry and Messrs. Sagoo and Takhar went on to emerge as two of the biggest and prominent family businesses in Southall and both continued to engage in and support the work of IWA. Mr. Chaudhry opened the first restaurant on The Broadway and Messrs. Sagoo and Takhar opened up the first Asian restaurants in 'Old' Southall next door to the Dominion Cinema.

The IWA, under the leadership of President Mr. Harbans Singh Ruprah and its General Secretary Vishnu Dutt Sharma, purchased the Dominion cinema in December 1965 for £75,000 from its owners, Associated British Cinemas. Initially the IWA experienced difficulty in raising this money as its bank only offered a loan of £30,000 towards the purchase price and IWA was unable to raise the remainder. However the IWA leadership approached the Indian Finance Minister who was in Britain to attend an International Finance Ministers' meeting. Through the support and intervention of the Indian Finance Minister, the bank agreed to loan IWA £50,000. The IWA raised the remaining £25,000 through a combination of interest free personal loans and donations from its members and the local community. Some individuals loaned as much as £1,000 to IWA and the IWA later repaid these loans to each and every member and supporter.

While the IWA managed the day to day running of the Dominion Cinema, it appointed independent Trustees to act as custodians of the Cinema and to avoid the Cinema being embroiled in its internal politics.

Mr. Ruprah, IWA President receiving keys of Dominion Cinema from IWA solicitor Mr. Hosteller, 1965

Dominion Cinema, 1968

Ajmer Singh Gill was appointed as the first Manager of Dominion Cinema and Parminder Singh Bal replaced him as the second Manager.

The IWA leadership and membership both wanted an independent base and a venue which could provide space for political, social and cultural activity for the growing Asian community in Southall.

The films generated huge income which IWA utilised to fund its social and cultural activity including Indian Independence Day celebrations, run its information advice and welfare service as well as its political campaigns and meetings.

At the beginning family members of IWA members did not have to pay entry fees and could see films free of charge. Later on IWA introduced ticket prices with a discounted rate for its members. At one time in the late 1960s, the ticket price for a film was around 3 shillings and 6 pence.

In response to the growing demand the Cinema started showing film shows on Saturdays and Sundays and later launched a film show for women only on Wednesday afternoons. By 1976, the Cinema began to attract an estimated 8,000 film goers on a weekly basis and the ticket price fluctuated around £1.

The Cinema achieved national and international acclaim and prominence and its popularity led the Indian film industry to use it to launch and release new films and many of Bollywood's greats made appearances at the Cinema and at these launches.

The Cinema became the main community hub for Asians and the IWA began hosting huge cultural and political events annually to commemorate Indian Independence Day, inviting prominent artists and musicians as well as speakers from the India diaspora, UK Government, trade union movement and prominent national politicians and bodies who wanted to engage with the Indian community.

The Cinema provided a national platform and IWA began organising events featuring classic and folk dances, poetry recitals, songs and performances by renowned artists from India and Britain. The Cinema's Ballroom began to be used for weddings and its boxing ring hosted wresting events, the most popular sport amongst Panjabi community and featured the legendary Panjabi and national Indian wrestling champion, Dara Singh, who performed to full houses.

(L-R): Messrs: K.Bhatia (IWA Welfare Officer), G. Dhillon, M. Padda, UK Government Immigration Minister, A.Rai, H.Ruprah, T.Toor, S. Malhi, M. Gill in Dominion cinema ticketing area

Ajit Rai addressing a political meeting at Dominion cinema ballroom with Dr. Basu, President of India League (L) and M. Padda (R)

DEMISE OF THE DOMINION CINEMA

While the purchase of Dominion Cinema heralded the beginning of a new era for the IWA, it was in equal measure responsible for posing a threat to the very survival of the organisation.

With technological advances and the advent of video films in the mid-970s, competition from two other local cinemas in Southall, 'The Liberty' and 'The Century' cinemas as well as a new cinema in Hanger Lane and other cinemas across London, cinema audiences plummeted nationally. The income from the Dominion Cinema began to decline and eventually its income crashed. The IWA was trapped in a situation where it had no option but to keep its Cinema open despite the substantial running costs to maintain the Cinema building along with retaining its large staff team. In addition the IWA was faced with the need to maintain its valuable Welfare service and offices which itself was financially dependent on the income generated from the Cinema. This situation spiralled from bad to worse with the IWA at one stage burdened with the costs of maintaining a non functional Cinema slowing deteriorating into a state of total disrepair on one hand and no audiences and income on the other hand.

In 1972, when Ajit Singh Rai (President) and Mohinder Singh Padda (General Secretary) assumed the IWA leadership after its 1972 elections, the IWA was in a relatively stable financial position and without any debt. However by the end of their tenure in 1977, the IWA had accumulated debts of an estimated £80,000. After the 1972 elections, the IWA became embroiled in legal wrangling and High Court action between the Ajit Rai grouping and its opposition, which was coordinated by Vishnu Sharma, and this legal dispute contributed to no elections being held for a further 3 years and until 1977.

After the 1977 elections, Vishnu Sharma (President) and Piara Khabra (General Secretary) assumed leadership and inherited a debt of around £80,000 from their predecessors. Even worse financial problems were to follow. Efforts by this new leadership to deal with IWA's massive debt problem were further strangulated by the interest accruing on the original debt itself. By the end of their own two-year tenure in October 1979, a toxic combination of lack of income, need to maintain a Welfare service and accumulating interest on the debt had increased the original debt to a staggering £120,000.

During this period the Cinema building had deteriorated and went into a state of total disrepair to such an extent that it became totally unusable. By 1980 the Cinema was closed with the exception of the rear of its building which continued to be used as the IWA Offices and to maintain its Welfare, advice and information services.

Faced with an unsurmountable and financially crippling debt problem, the IWA leadership began to contemplate the issue of the sale and lease of the Cinema site to the local Council. This created divisions and acrimonious political disputes between the IWA leadership and its various 'opposition' groups, most of which viewed the Dominion Cinema as the 'mother' of IWA, could not countenance its sale and considered its sale as a betrayal of the community and an 'existential' threat to the IWA.

On 23rd December 1982, faced with a mounting and crippling debt and accumulating daily interest charges, the IWA leadership was finally forced to make a deal and lease the Dominion

Urdu Poet *Mirza Ghalib Centenary* in Dominion cinema.
From L to R: Darshan Singh Giani, Film Director Ravi, unknown, Om Prakash, Dilip Kumar, Deputy High Commissioner Kaul, Nargis, Sunil Dutt, Wahida Rahman, Mehtab, Urdu Poet Kanwir, Mohinder Singh Bedi, Gurmukh Singh Musafar MP (India), Panjabi writer & former Panjab Chief Minister

Cinema building to Ealing Council for a term of 99 years. As part of this deal the Council paid off the IWA's estimated debt of £120,000, agreed to build IWA an independent IWA building and office base and make a one off payment of £50,000 which was to be held in a non- cashable bond by the IWA for 5 years.

The Cinema was demolished and turned into a Community Centre, initially managed by a Management Committee of nominated representatives of Ealing Council and elected local community and user representatives. The IWA was given a guaranteed and automatic place on the new Centre's Management Committee.

In 2081, this entire current Community Centre site, which now also incorporates the new Southall Library, will revert back to IWA ownership and the IWA's future generation of leaders will inherit a multi-million pound asset.

Mirza Ghalib Centenary event in Dominion cinema.
From L to R: Unknown, Om Prakash, Darshan Singh Giani, Dilip Kumar, Deputy High Commissioner Kaul, Nargis, Wahida Rahman, Mohinder Singh Bedi, Gurmukh Singh Musafar MP (India), Panjabi writer and former Panjab Chief Minister

IWA WELFARE SERVICES

During the years prior to 1956, an informal network of educated Indians, fluent in English or with a background of social and political activism in India, organised and provided support to newly arriving immigrants, almost exclusively men from the Indian sub-continent. This network included individuals who laid the foundation for the formation of IWA Southall and who were to become key members of the first IWA Executive Committee.

The majority of newly arriving immigrants had little or no knowledge of English making even the most basic daily tasks such as filling in a job application form, using public transportation, shopping, registering with a doctor, writing letters to families back home etc, extremely onerous, difficult and impossible without help. Anecdotal evidence recounts many tales whereby some elders would leave visible signs or items, outside their houses or on their streets, in order to identify where they lived and to find or navigate their way back home. Understanding and dealing with an array of different public institutions and local services could not be undertaken without support from their 'educated' countrymen. Their plight was made worse by the fact that many of them had arrived using forged passports and documentation, which made them more vulnerable to exploitation and reluctant to approach local services.

By 1957, IWA Southall's network of founding members and supporters was effectively operating a welfare service through holding activity at Southall Community Centre on Bridge Road, Southall, every weekend. This regular activity enabled local Indians to come together socially, access Indian newspapers and basic English language classes as well as seek information and advice. IWA activists routinely accompanied people wishing to find out about or access basic public services, acting as interpreters, translators and advocates.

By 1962, the Asian population in Southall had increased substantially and the demand for IWA's welfare services had become overwhelming and it recognised the need for the IWA to establish an independent base from which to coordinate its various welfare and political activity. In September 1962, under the leadership of Harbans Ruprah and Vishnu Sharma, the IWA opened its Welfare Centre and Reading Room on 18 Featherstone Road, which was part of the local Working Men's Club building. The IWA Welfare Centre became the first and only Centre where Asians could go to seek assistance and support on any issue they faced. Over the coming two decades the Centre became a local landmark and supported tens of thousands of people, on issues ranging from basic reading of letters from loved ones back home, accessing basic rights and public services to advocacy and legal representation in complex immigration cases.

The main areas of concern and support focused on dealing with problems and issues related to forged passports and irregular status of workers, immigration, taxation, accessing basic rights or public services such as education and housing, discrimination in employment, bringing families and spouses from India into Britain. Translation and interpreting support undermined all support services.

The social and welfare activity at this Centre included English Language classes and other activity particularly for the growing number of Asian women who were by now coming to join their husbands, space for social gatherings, a Reading Room with access to Indian newspapers

Opening of IWA Offices, 18 Featherstone Road
(L-R) Messrs: M.Gill, G.Dhillon, S. Malhi, H. Ruprah, A.Rai, UK Government Immigration Minister, T. Toor, P. Padda, S. Bidwell MP, K.Bhatia (IWA Welfare Officer)

along with celebrations to commemorate key Indian events such as Indian Independence Day and Diwali.

In response to the demand for its Welfare services, the IWA appointed one Male and one Female Welfare Officer. The first full time and paid IWA Welfare Officer, Mr. Om Dogra, started employment in 1964 and was based at its offices on 18 Featherstone Road. Mr Krishan Bhatia, was appointed as Welfare Officer in 1974.

During the tenure of Ajit Rai and Mohinder Padda as President and General Secretary, the IWA began the practice of appointing its General Secretary as a full-time paid post. Mohinder Padda became the first full time and paid IWA General Secretary in 1973. Thereafter the practice of the IWA's General Secretary or President acting and working as its full-time paid Officer became an accepted and established practice.

In 1979, the IWA moved its offices and Welfare services from 18 Featherstone Road premises to the rear of its Dominion Cinema. In 1983 with the closure and transfer of the Dominion Cinema to Ealing Council on a 99 year lease, the IWA Welfare services and office was relocated temporarily to Southall Town Hall. By this time the IWA had established a nationally acclaimed immigration advice service which was regarded as one of the best in the country.

In 1987, the IWA's Welfare service and main office was finally relocated back to its new building, which had been specifically built for it by Ealing Council as part of the redevelopment of the old Dominion Cinema site, at 112 The Green, Southall and adjacent to the new and redeveloped Dominion Community Centre. Neil Kinnock, MP and Leader of the Labour Party visited and opened this new IWA building in January 1988.

Throughout the 1970s, 1980s and 1990s, the IWA delivered support to tens of thousands of people from across the country annually.

In 1986, IWA set up its first publically funded projects, Southall Community Service along with an Environment Project, which between them employed 36 staff and 3 supervisors. The IWA utilised these project to encourage and support local unemployed people to enter the world of work and to support other local community and voluntary sector organisations.

Piara Singh Khabra, IWA President, like his predecessor, Sardul Singh Gill before him, became a Justice of the Peace (JP) and in that capacity personally provided one of the most valued and free service through the offices of the IWA. As JPs, both were able to witness or countersign documentation which would otherwise have required thousands of people to go before a solicitor and pay a fee to have the same documents formally attested. Providing free access to such a service via a JP at the offices of the IWA became an essential and established part of IWA's public service and elevated the position of JPs within the local community. This subsequently encouraged many other Asians to become a JP.

From 1975 to 1977 around 500 people visited the IWA Welfare Centre and Reading Room which provided all the daily Indian newspapers in English, Panjabi and Urdu including Daily Tribune, Daily Patriot, Daily Milap, Daily Ajit, Daily Zamane, Daily Quami Dard and Daily Lok Lehar.

IWA Office Opening Ceremony by UK Government Immigration Minister, 18 Featherstone Road

Indian Government Ministers including Darwara Singh and Gurdial Singh (R: 6th & 7th) with IWA members

From 1975 to 1977, the IWA provided information advice and support to thousands of people as follows:
- Immigration (2,000)
- Immigration appeals (94)
- Industrial appeals (20)
- Income Tax (200)
- Passports (276)
- Airport Detentions (89)

IWA distributed 1000s of free forms on sponsorships, finances, accommodation certificates, passport, renewal of passports, extension of stay, revoking of conditions after marriages of fiancés/fiancées coming on limited period stays, regularisation of stay for overstayers and illegal entrants, change of names etc.

From May 1983 to April 1985, IWA dealt with 24,078 cases:
- Declarations and Sponsorships (5,713)
- Indian Passport Service (4,635)
- Documentation (3,178)
- General Information (4,173)
- Immigration (2,675)
- Affidavits (1,518)

INDIAN PASSPORT AND VISA SERVICE

The IWA's position as the leading organisation of people from the Indian diaspora outside of India was recognised and endorsed by the Indian High Commission in London, which had a 'special relationship' with IWA since its inception. The Indian High Commission conferred to IWA a special status, whereby IWA was authorised to provide a weekly 'Indian Passport and Indian Visa Service' to the Indian community in Britain. Through this Service, any person of Indian origin was able to submit and have their applications for Indian passports, passport renewals and Indian visas processed through the IWA. Applicants were supported and able to have all the relevant documentation assembled and attested at the IWA offices and later collect their new passports or visas from the IWA, without having to make the journey to the Indian High Commission in central London. The IWA would take all the passports and applications to Indian High Commission on a weekly basis, deal with and resolve any enquires with the High Commission officials, bring back properly endorsed passports and return them to their owners.

This service was invaluable particularly to older people who faced difficulties with commuting to Indian High Commission's offices in Aldwych central London and others who either could not deal with the cumbersome bureaucracy, official obstinacy and persistent delays associated in the working of the Indian High Commission and its officials. The IWA's expertise ensured that all correct documentation and all responses to potential enquiries were prepared and its staff acted as conduits to resolving complicated cases. The IWA's close relationship with the Indian High Commission was such that it operated a direct 'hot line' whereby it could contact senior officials at the High Commission and deal with and resolve individual cases immediately including urgent and complex cases within a matter of hours.

This service was effectively terminated when Indian High Commission outsourced its Indian Passports and Visa Service to the private sector.

VIRGINITY TESTS ON ASIAN WOMEN FROM INDIAN SUB-CONTINENT AT HEATHROW AIRPORT

Under the Immigration Act 1971, stricter controls operated against Asian men wishing to settle in the UK on the basis of marriage. However the similar restrictions were not applicable on Asian women. Asian women coming to the UK to marry fiancés did not need a visa if their marriage was to be held within a period of 3 months in the UK. Unlike immigrant men, who were deemed to have an immediate economic value as unskilled or skilled labour, immigrant women from the Indian sub-continent were viewed by successive British Governments as having no value in the labour market.

'Virginity Testing' was effectively an immigration 'control' measure designed and targeted at making it difficult for women, particularly fiancés and married women from the Indian sub-continent, to enter Britain. The degrading inhumane and racist practice of 'Virginity Tests' by immigration officers at UK airports and at British High Commissions in India, Pakistan and Bangladesh was exposed as a result of a 'medical examination' conducted on a 35-year old Indian woman, by a male doctor, wishing to enter the UK to marry her fiancé, a British subject of Indian origin at Heathrow Airport on 24th January 1979.

Immigration officers carried out 'virginity tests', an invasive gynaecological examination, on Asian fiancés who wished to enter the UK on the basis of marrying spouses already settled in the UK, to establish whether these women had previously borne children and were virgins. The outcome of these 'virginity tests' was used to refuse entry to Asian women into the UK.

The Labour Government initially denied the existence or the practice of 'virginity tests' but were forced to accept the existence of this practice following a public confirmation from a former Labour Party Immigration Minister, Alex Lyons. Alex Lyons' statement to the media confirmed that he had discovered the practice of 'virginity tests' was commonplace and being used as early as in October 1975 in British High Commissions in South Asia and that he had ordered that this practice be stopped while he was a Minister.

The IWA immediately launched and spearheaded a massive national opposition campaign and made representations to the Indian Government. The Indian Government, led by Prime Minister Moraji Desai, protested to the Labour Government led by Prime Minister Jim Callaghan. The Indian Government, outraged at this practice, also took the matter to the UN Commission on Human Rights.

The British Government accepted that since October 1975, there had been 9 cases of 'virginity testing' in Bombay and 73 cases in New Delhi and announced the termination of this practice.

Evidence of 81 cases of 'virginity testing' was later found in the Home Office's confidential files. It is believed that these 81 cases were only the tip of the iceberg and that hundreds of Asian women had been subjected to this appalling, dehumanising and racist practice.

Vishnu Sharma speaking at IWA public meeting at Dominion cinema

Indian Independence Day commemoration and political meeting at Dominion cinema

MURDER OF CHAGGAR: 4th June 1976

On 4th June 1976, Gurdip Singh Chaggar, a local student was stabbed to death by racists opposite the Dominion Cinema and in front of The Victory Pub on The Green, Southall, in the heart of the Asian community.

The Asian community, particularly young people, outraged by racial violence and the lack of response to racist attacks from the police erupted in anger, staging incidents of sporadic civil opposition and protest. Young people vociferously voiced their anger and criticisms against the established 'community leaders', principally as represented by the IWA and the local Gurdwaras and other faith organisations, for their inaction. In the ensuing protests a number of young people were arrested and this led to hundreds of Asian young people laying siege to Southall Police Station, organising a mass sit -down, demanding the unconditional release of all those arrested.

The IWA leadership along with other 'community leaders' acted as chief negotiators with the Police on the release of those arrested and taken to Southall Police Station in order to diffuse the situation.

The IWA subsequently led and coordinated meetings to bring together different interests, unify community responses and organised a Peace March in Southall which was attended by thousands of local residents, other sympathisers and anti-racists from across the country.

The murder of Gurdip Chaggar had exposed the growing schism between the younger generation of Asians and the 'old and established guards' and community 'leaders'. It was a defining moment when young Asians organised themselves and established the Southall Youth Movement (SYM).

In 1983, Balraj Purewal one of the founder members and General Secretary of SYM, was to be embraced by the IWA leadership under Piara Khabra. Balraj Purewal went on to became Assistant General Secretary of the IWA and later in 1985, after the murder of Tarsem Singh Toor, became General Secretary of IWA.

Scene of murder of Gurdip Chaggar outside The Victory Pub, The Green, June 1976

Young people erupting in anger on aftermath of murder of Gurdip Chaggar, June 1976

NATIONAL FRONT MEETING in Southall Town Hall: The Murder of Blair Peach, 23 April 1979

The National Front (NF) was widely known for and associated within immigrant communities for its racist and vitriolic hatred of black immigrants and an organisation which openly espoused a policy of deportation of black immigrants.

The NF fielded John Fairhurst as its candidate in Southall in the May 1979 General Election. From the outset it was clear that the NF would not secure votes in a predominately immigrant constituency and that its proposal to hold a meeting at Southall Town Hall was a deliberate and provocative strategy to divide communities and gain publicity.

The IWA organised mass mobilisation, coordinating and leading opposition, urging the Conservative controlled Ealing Council to refuse NF permission to meet in Southall Town Hall.

The IWA under the leadership of Vishnu Sharma its President, set up a Coordinating Committee bringing together all local organisations at a meeting at Dominion Cinema on 11 April 1979. It also organised a mass demonstration and March to Ealing Town Hall on 22 April 1979 in which 5,000 people took part. It also presented a petition with 10,000 signatures to Ealing Council to refuse permission to NF to host any meeting in Southall, urging the Council to provide the NF an alternative venue elsewhere. The IWA simultaneously urged that 'all businesses, restaurants, shops, etc. should shut down on 23 April from 1 p.m. onwards' as a mark of protest.

In spite of widespread community opposition, supported by national bodies such at the Commission for Racial Equality, the churches and others, the Conservative controlled Ealing Council decided to allow the racist NF to hold a public meeting in Southall Town Hall on 23 April 1979 under the pretext of and citing the rights of 'political parties' to hold meetings under the General Election rules, which were due in May 1979.

The IWA promoted protest in the form a 'Hartal' (a common protest in the form of civil disobedience used in the Indian freedom struggles) and decided 'not to resort to confrontation with the police' and planned a 'massive peaceful sit-down' outside Southall Town Hall.

The NF meeting was scheduled to begin at 7.30pm and the IWA's 'sit- down' was planned for 5pm. However the protests organised by the Southall Youth Movement had started by midday on that day and had escalated into open confrontations between police and local young people by around 3pm. With huge number of police officers deployed, the police and the Special Patrol Group, began preventing young people and local community from protesting outside or anywhere near the vicinity of Southall Town Hall. Police set up cordons around Southall Town Hall and the whole of central Southall was effectively sealed off by 3pm, resulting in several hundred local residents stranded outside these cordons and not even allowed to go back to their own homes.

2,875 police officers were deployed (including 94 on horseback) to protect the NF's right of assembly and against the interests and wishes of the whole community.

Blair Peach, a teacher and an anti-racist, who had come to Southall in support of the community was killed by police and over 800 protesters were arrested and many injured.

The body of Blair Peach was laid in repose at the IWA's Dominion Cinema, with a guard of honour from members of Southall Youth Movement. An estimated 10,000 people paid homage

Young people staging sit-down opposite Southall Police Station, June 1976

Memorial marchers go past the place where Blair Peach was killed, 1979

to Blair Peach.

On 28 April 1979, the IWA organised a March through Southall, attended by approximately 15,000 people, in memory of Blair Peach.

The IWA coordinated and launched a Defence Committee and a Defence Fund to raise money to support those arrested and charged during the protests.

On 23rd April 1979, 2,875 police officers were deployed (including 94 on horseback).

Over 800 protesters were arrested,

342 were charged.

Blair Peach, was killed by police.

A special Stipendiary Court was set up in Barnet to hear the cases.

Peace and Unity March in memory of the murders of Gurdip Chaggar and Blair Peach

IWA delegates along with SYM representatives and others in front of 10 Downing Street delivering Memorandum after Gurdip Chaggar's murder, June 1976

IWA AND PUBLIC FUNDING

From its very inception, the IWA's founding members ardently believed in and were committed to the IWA being an autonomous and independent organisation and repudiated any form of state aid or other public funding towards its work, on the basis that it would compromise its independence.

Until the early 1980s, the IWA's social and welfare services along with its political activity remained resourced exclusively through income generated by donations from the local community and businesses, membership fees and ticket sales from the Dominion Cinema.

It was not until the mid-1980s that the IWA first ventured into operating a publically funded service through participating in a national government funded Manpower Services Commission (MSC) Programme targeted at supporting local unemployed people. Under this MSC Programme, the IWA managed a Community Scheme which employed 20 local unemployed people, who were involved in providing support beneficial to local community and organisations. In 1986, the IWA was managing three MSC funded projects providing employment to unemployed local people; a Welfare Project, its Southall Community Support Project and an Environment Project which between them employed a total of 35 workers including 3 supervisors.

Balraj Purewal, one of the new and younger generation of community activists who first became involved in IWA in 1983, drove IWA's first real venture to secure public funding for its own core work to consolidate the colossal work and benefit the IWA was delivering to communities.

The IWA's first grant application was made to the Greater London Council (GLC) for the costs of appointing a Director to act as the IWA's central officer and to coordinate its activities. Though the GLC awarded a grant to the IWA, it did not approve of IWA's policy and working model of appointing its elected General Secretary or President as its full-time worker, arguing that such a policy ran contrary to the GLC's guidelines particularly around conflicts of interests and recruitment. The divisions between the IWA and the GLC ultimately led to the grant to IWA being withdrawn in 1989.

The IWA, working in collaboration with Focus Consultancy, also secured a one-year contract from the Department of Health to engage in a research project on HIV and AIDS within the Asian communities in Southall. This work was coordinated by a community based Steering Group, led by Balraj Purewal and Tuku Mukherjee, which operated under the auspices of the IWA. This Steering Group organised research on HIV and AIDS amongst the Sikh community in Southall and presented its positon paper to the Department of Health and its advisors. The Department of Health found the IWA's critique of its own strategy and practice unacceptable and forthwith terminated the IWA's contract.

Tuku Mukherjee subsequently produced a publication 'Living in Terror', a critique of HIV and AIDS related debate, work and strategies in Britain in 1993.

In 1986, the IWA secured a grant for a Community Development Officer post from London Borough of Ealing and by 1987 it had secured a second grant from London Borough of Hounslow for a similar post in Hounslow. This latter grant led IWA to open an office at 10 School Road, Hounslow, in 1988 and these grants led to the appointment of two Community Development

Officers. Sukhwant Singh Sandher and Kamaljit Kaur Johal were appointed and served as the first Community Development Officers for Ealing and Hounslow respectively.

The IWA was instrumental in influencing Hounslow Council to set up the first Asian Elders Day Centre at Wellington Road through it Hounslow based work.

IWA ANTI-RACISM TRAINING PROGRAMMES AND PUBLICATIONS

In the mid-1980s the IWA began to recognise the need to organise activity to address racial discrimination and institutional racism within public sector institutions, policies and practices. This new focus and approach within IWA's work was driven by Balraj Purewal, its Assistant General Secretary at the time, who had previously been involved with the Southall Youth Movement and had a history of and commitment to anti-racist interventions.

In 1985, Balraj Purewal produced one of the first IWA booklets on national policy, a critique of Section 11 of the Local Government Act 1966, arguing against the racist premise on which the Government had based this policy on and the abuse of Section 11 resources allocated to local authorities under this legislation.

In 1986, the IWA organised the first of its numerous Anti-Racism Training Programmes which was held at its new offices on 112 The Green. This 3 day training programme was a pioneering interventionist educational programme, devised and facilitated by Tuku Mukherjee, and initially targeted at professionals working within the public sector, particularly education and social services. The IWA's first training programme attracted 16 participants each paying £25 to attend this programme.

A Collective led by Tuku Mukherjee and supported by Balraj Purewal from the IWA, was formed and in April 1987 its work culminated in the first IWA Conference specifically targeted at public sector professionals which was held at the Dominion Centre. This Conference was a landmark for the IWA as it was the first time IWA had organised a Conference which charged participants a fee to attend. The Conference fee was £85 per delegate and approximately 100 professional delegates from across the country, representing a range of governmental, independent and community bodies attended.

The Conference was simultaneously used to launch the IWA's first publication entitled: 'The Regeneration of Racism: Hypocrisy of Inner City Policies', written by the Collective led by Tuku Mukherjee.

The words 'Black' and 'Immigrant' don't only stir a world of feelings, attitudes and behaviour but generate resources to create structures and maintain a distorted definition of immigrants as 'disadvantaged' and 'problematic'.
Tuku Mukherjee: IWA advisor and educationalist

BLACK INNER CITY UPRISINGS

the REGENERATION of RACISM

Hypocrisy of Inner City Policies

Indian Workers' Association
Southall

NATIONAL AND INTERNATIONAL WORK AND CAMPAIGNS

From its inception to the mid-1980s, IWA was undoubtedly one of the leading and nationally acclaimed organisation within the Asian, African Caribbean and Refugee communities and recognised by successive governments as the authentic voice and representative of the immigrant community. Throughout the decades, IWA actively engaged in numerous strategic national working groups and committees to influence central government policy on immigration, community and race relations.

Joint Council for the Welfare of Immigrants (JCWI)

Vishnu Sharma was one of the co-founders of the JCWI, the leading national body specialising in and campaigning on immigration, nationality and asylum issues. The inaugural meeting to set up the JCWI was held in the Dominion Cinema, Southall, in 1967 and on its establishment Vishnu Sharma was elected as its first General Secretary.

Vishnu Sharma subsequently worked for JCWI for 11 years, forging close links between IWA and JCWI, which led to collaborative working and joint campaigns over several decades on immigration, race relations and nationality matters.

Coordinating Committee Against Racial Discrimination (CCARD)

IWA was instrumental in setting up CCARD, a national alliance and an umbrella group for all the major organisations fighting against discrimination in Britain in the 1960s.

Vishnu Sharma and Harjinder Dhillon of IWA were Vice-Chair and National Treasurer of CCARD respectively.

National Council for Commonwealth of Immigrants (NCCI)

IWA was represented within NCCI, the forerunner of the Commission for Racial Equality until 1968, when Vishnu Sharma, the IWA representative, resigned in protest at the introduction of the Immigration Act 1968.

Race Relations Board and Race Relations Act 1965

The IWA worked at various levels in different committees which led or contributed to the development of both the Race Relations Board and the first Race Relations Act, to tackle racial discrimination in this country.

UK Amnesty for Illegal Immigrants

The IWA lobbied and worked with successive governments to secure an Amnesty for all illegal immigrants and others exploited by virtue of their irregular immigration status.

IWA's national campaign resulted in the Government announcing an Amnesty for Commonwealth citizens and citizens of Pakistan, who entered illegally on or after 9 March 1968, which came into effect on 1 January 1973.

The Amnesty was the culmination of one of the most important and effective campaigns organised by the IWA in Britain.

Indian Independence Day celebrations and political Rally featuring (L-R) Mr. Khangura, Mr. Khabra, Indian High Commissioner, Mr. Binder, Mr. Ruprah, Shourie, John McDonnel MP

Asian leader hits out at race Bill

THE Government's nationality Bill has been attacked as racialist by Southall Indian Workers Association President Piara Khabra.

Mr Khabra said if the Bill becomes law Asian people in England will have to fight and it will encourage the racialist elements in the community.

He said: "The Bill will take away the rights of many people already settled here.

"People in certain categories will definitely be debarred from holding offices in government departments and some industries."

Senior law lecturer Mr Charles Blake, who works at Ealing College, said the Bill's proposals on marrying a UK citizen could seriously affect the Asian community.

At the moment a woman marrying a U.K. citizen is automatically entitled to U.K. citizenship, while a man is not.

In future, neither wife or husband will be entitled to citizenship, as of right, on marriage.

The spouse will have to qualify by natrualization but after three years instead of five.

Mr Blake said the language test on naturalization will also make it harder for Asians to qualify.

Another proposal is that Commonwealth citizens who settled here before 1973 and have been resident since, can as of right register as U.K. citizens.

At present, Commonwealth citizens settled here after 1973 can apply for citizenship at the discretion of the Home Secretary after five years ordinary residence. Such citizenship passes by descent, through a father, to children even if birth takes place abroad.

The definition of "ordinary residence" will be tightened and will include specific periods of living here and specific periods of permitted absence.

It will no longer be possible to transmit citizenship by descent where the parent has moved on since registering and the birth of a child takes place abroad. The only exception will be if the absence abroad is temporary.

If the child settles in the U.K. with its parents it will become entitled to citizenship after three years.

At present any child born in the U.K. acquires U.K. citizenship even if their parents have no link with the country. For example, if they are here on holiday.

So a child born in the U.K. to parents who are not U.K. citizens and whose stay here is not free of conditions, will not acquire U.K. citizenship by birth.

This could affect a person here on a work permit or who overstays or who breaks a condition of stay.

But a birth to parents who are settled here, even if they are not U.K. citizens, will still confer U.K. citizenship on the child.

Mr Blake said the new Act would probably not come into force until about 1982.

Vietnam War

The IWA organised meetings against the Vietnam War and mobilised public support for the people of North Vietnam and their struggles. IWA openly opposed the American intervention in Vietnam and its policy of 'carpet bombing' which indiscriminately killed thousands of civilians.

The capture of Saigon in April 1975 by the North Vietnamese marked the end of this war and resulted in the reunification of North and South Vietnam.

Indian Dual Nationality Campaign

IWA was for decades in the forefront of the international campaign on Dual Nationality, pressing successive Indian governments to confer dual nationality on Non-Resident Indians (NRIs) living in UK and other countries. IWA representations to successive Indian Government officials focused on NRIs' inextricable links with India through land and property ownership, family and business relationships and investments, the economic value of the foreign currency remittances made by NRIs and the need for NRIs involved in land and property disputes to be protected and treated as equal citizens within Indian legislation and courts.

IWA played a critical part in the Indian Government's decision to confer the special status of 'People of Indian Origin' (PIO) and later 'Overseas Citizen of India' (OCI) on NRIs.

Harassment of Non-Resident Indians (NRIs) at Indian Ports of Entry

The IWA consistently protested and raised the issue of the harassment and onerous inspections by zealous immigration officials, intent on extorting money or goods from visiting NRIs at Delhi, Mumbai, Amritsar and other Indian ports of entry. This pressure eventually led to better treatment of NRIs at ports of entry.

Expulsion of East African Asians from Uganda

0n 4 August 1972, Idi Amin, President of Uganda, ordered the expulsion of Asians giving them 90 days to leave Uganda. 50,000 Asians were expelled from Uganda and Britain took 27,200 refugees as many of these Ugandan Indians were citizens of the UK and the Colonies.

The IWA supported the resettlement of these new refugees, raised funds, coordinated temporary accommodation along with information, advice and other support. It actively collaborated with Gujarati community leaders and organisations across the country as well as with other national agencies to coordinate relief and support and on issues affecting resettlement.

Poll Tax Campaign

The 'Poll Tax', as it became known, introduced by the Conservative Government led by Margaret Thatcher in 1987, imposed a single flat rate per capita tax on each adult living in any house and replaced the tax previously levied on an individual property.

The IWA campaigned, organising petitions, holding meetings and a regular stall on The

IWA Conference of Overseas Indians on Dual Nationality Chaired by Piara Khabra (2nd Right) and Lord Navnit Dholakia, President of Liberal Democrats from 2001-2004 (3rd Right)

Delegates attending IWA Conference of Overseas Indians on Dual Nationality at Dominion cinema

Broadway for months, to mobilise public support for the abolition of this draconian tax. IWA campaigned that the 'Poll Tax' would have a disproportionate and discriminatory impact on Asian households, which were extended family households and hence comprised of larger numbers of adults living in them.

The 'Poll Tax' was finally abandoned after national opposition which culminated in a number of Poll Tax riots, including the most serious one, during a protest in Trafalgar Square London, which more than 200,000 protestors attended.

Section 11: Local Government Act 1966
Under Section 11, millions of pounds of state aid were made available to those local authorities which had 'substantial numbers of immigrants from the Commonwealth'. By the mid-1980s, the Section 11 annual budget had reached around £100 million. IWA campaigned against the abuse of Section 11 funding by local authorities and pressed for community groups to be given direct access to Section 11 funding.

The IWA published a critique of Section 11 funding in 1990 and its work contributed to the Government's decision to allow 'secondments' of staff employed under Section 11 to community and voluntary sector agencies.

British Nationality 1981
This Act came into effect on 1 January 1983 and created 3 separate types of citizenships, namely British Citizen, British Dependent Territories Citizenship and British Overseas Citizenship. The Act created panic amongst citizens with Indian passports and with passports from other Commonwealth countries, who feared that they would have no option but to acquire British nationality or lose basic rights including their right to live or vote in Britain. It led to a massive surge in applications to register to become British citizens as the deadline for application approached on 31 December 1987.

IWA was inundated with appeals for help and supported thousands of people to acquire British nationality through a process of Naturalisation or Registration.

International Delegations
IWA delegation of Ajit Rai, Harbans Ruprah and Tarsem Toor went to India in November 1975 and met with Indian Prime Minister Indira Gandhi , Minister of External Affairs (Mr Swaran Singh), Defence Minister (Mr. C. Subramanium), Finance Minister (Pranab Mukherjee), as well as leaders of all the main political parties including CPI leaders, Giani Zail Singh (Chief Minister of Panjab) on issues concerning Non Resident Indians and to give their views on the State of Emergency imposed by the Indira Gandhi's Government across India.

The IWA delegation also attended the International Conference Against Fascism held in Patna in December 1975.

An IWA delegation of Ajit Rai and Mohinder Padda went to Brussels and met EEC

(L-R): Messrs:.Shourie, Toor and Dhillon in discussion with Mrs. Indira Gandhi, Prime Minister of India

(L-R) Messrs: Toor, Rai, Padda and Ruprah in a private meeting with Mrs. Indira Gandhi, Prime Minister of India in her Office in New Delhi

Commissioners as part of the IWA's campaign against Britain's entry into the Common Market on the grounds that British entry would impact adversely against the interests of Commonwealth immigrants and working class workers and to influence EEC to safeguard the interests of immigrants.

Political Rallies and Meeting

The IWA has coordinated, led or participated in innumerable national demonstrations, meetings, conferences and political rallies. From the 1960s to the 1980s its social and political events gained a formidable political reputation, base and attracted many delegations. Many prominent British and Indian politicians, trade union leaders and international activists attended its meetings and regarded IWA as the most important and powerful organisation representing the interests of people from the Indian sub-continent and as a conduit to engaging with immigrant communities.

Some of these prominent politicians to have attended IWA's political rallies have included:

Indira Gandhi (Prime Minister of India); Rahul Gandhi (Prime Minister of India); Swaran Singh (Indian Foreign Affairs Minister) along with Defence and other Ministers of Government of India; Successive Chief Ministers of Panjab; Sant Fateh Singh (one of the Leaders of Panjabi Suba Movement); Douglas Hume (Minister in Conservative Government); Michael Foot and Neil Kinnock (Leaders of Labour Party); Dennis Healy (Labour Government Minister); Tony Benn along with various Immigration Ministers of UK Govt: Lord Fenner Brockway and other prominent officials and dignitaries.

In recognition of the IWA's powerful position and importance, it became customary for potential new appointees to British High Commission in Delhi and Indian High Commissioners posted to London, to meet with IWA prior to their appointments.

Messrs: P. Khabra and H.Ruprah (centre) in discussion with Rahul Gandhi, Prime Minister of India

(L-R): R.Perdesi, H. Takhar, S.Gill, Dennis Healy (Labour Defence Minister) and D. Singh Giani at Indian High Commission, London

D.S.Giani and H. Dhillion with Mrs. Indira Gandhi, Prime Minister of India and Mr Dhawan, Indian High Commissione,: Dominion cinema, January 1969

SECTION 4

This Section provides an insight into the politics of the IWA (Southall), its membership, election process and groups competing for leadership positions.

IWA: MEMBERSHIP

In 1956, the membership fee was 2 shilling and 6 pence and the IWA founder members would go house to house, often spending days convincing their countrymen, friends, relatives and local Asian workers to become members of their new organisation.

The IWA had both Ordinary and Associate members and membership was available to any Indian which it defined as *'a person born in India or of parents and grandparents of Indian origin'* aged 18 years and over.

Over the coming decades, the membership fee was steadily increased to 5 shillings, £1 and by 2016 it was set at £5. Life membership was available for £10 (2016 fee) and the IWA recruited a significant number of Life members, most of whom took out this membership primarily during the 1960s and 1970s.

On 8th March 1966, IWA was formally registered as a Working Men's Club under the Friendly Societies Act 1896. Under this constitution, membership was made available to all people of Indian origin and resident in London Boroughs of Ealing, Hounslow, Hillingdon, Brent, Hammersmith and Fulham as well as in Colnbrook. At registration its membership fee was increased to 10 Shillings.

From around 1960, recruitment of members began to be organised by a wider circle of founder members, local activists and other individuals who had directly benefited from IWA advice and information and other welfare support services. Over the coming years many beneficiaries of its welfare service became members as a mark of respect and in appreciation of the support provided to them. During the early 1960s the income from membership fees became a vital source of income to sustain IWA's work and consequently membership recruitment became an important part of its strategy to generate income, in addition to engaging more local people in the organisation.

By the mid-1960s, IWA had become an established local and national body with a growing reputation for addressing the issues facing immigrant communities, campaigning for the rights of immigrant communities in Britain and providing valuable welfare services to members and non-members alike. IWA membership became increasing attractive amongst beneficiaries of its services and its reputation inevitably attracted more politically aspiring individuals and interest groups to become actively engaged in the policies, public services, political direction and overall management of the IWA.

From the mid-1960s to the mid-1970s, the numbers of 'politically active' individuals interested in or contesting the IWA leadership positions increased markedly and the recruitment and mobilisation of members, primarily based on village and family relationships, became established. It also became a common practice for potential aspiring leadership contenders to pay the membership fees of the individuals they were recruiting as IWA members, particularly during election periods.

During the 1970s, the IWA had established itself as a household name in Southall. The process and scale of the elections for its Executive Committee positions was phenomenal and unrivalled by any other organisation that existed in Britain at that time. Council elections to elect local ward councillors in Southall and Hounslow paled into insignificance within the Asian community in comparison to IWA elections, with far higher numbers of Asians participating and voting in the IWA elections than in the Council elections.

Individuals active in recruiting members along with prospective election candidates or future contenders became strategic players through using their own membership base to build influence and as a bargaining tool, to secure a position for themselves within a group or faction seeking to contest IWA elections.

In 1965, it is estimated that 3,000 Indians voted in the IWA elections, an estimated 75% of its members and around half the adult Indian male population in Southall at the time

In the 1968 election, a staggering 105 candidates contested 21 Executive Committee positions and IWA had an estimated 6,000 members. In 1976, IWA membership was in excess of 10,000 members.

At the beginning of 1979, IWA membership was nearly 15,000 but with one of the most hotly contested elections in 1979 and 1983, IWA membership reached a peak and went over 20,000 for the first time in its history. At these elections members voted at 3 venues across Ealing and Hounslow boroughs (2 in Southall and one in Cranford, Hounslow) to facilitate the numbers wanting the opportunity to vote.

EXECUTIVE COMMITTEE STRUCTURE

As the membership grew exponentially over the decades with the growth in the Indian population, the drive to become an Executive Committee (EC) member became extremely popular due to the perceived esteem and prominence which holding an official EC position created amongst candidates. Within the community being an EC member was synonymous with and a 'marker' of being a leading community figurehead or 'community leader'. The higher the official position an individual held within the hierarchical EC structure, the more powerful one was considered amongst the IWA rank and file membership as well as within the wider community. The positions of President and General Secretary became the most coveted positions, symbolising power, prestige and standing within the community.

The IWA elections were unparalleled political events conducted in fanfare and events bigger than the Council elections in Southall. Members could contest and stand for any of the 21 EC positions available which included 11 Officer posts namely post of President, Vice President, General Secretary, Deputy Secretary, Office Secretary, Financial Secretary, Cultural Secretary, Education Secretary, Propaganda Secretary, Welfare Secretary and Sports Secretary. In additional 10 Executive Committee Ordinary member positions were available. These positions and titles have barely changed over the decades. However, later on the post of Propaganda Secretary deleted and the number of EC members increased from 10 to 11. In 1989, the constitution was changed and the EC was renamed the Executive Council and the post of President was renamed as the Chairperson.

Such was the aspiration and ambition to be part of the IWA Executive Committee that prospective candidates clamoured to secure a position other than being just an Ordinary member of the EC. The titles eventually secured or bestowed upon prospective candidates were viewed as being reflective of their political stature and standing in the local community, let alone within the IWA's membership. It became a common practice for individuals who had previously served as EC Officers or Ordinary members but were no longer in power to 'hold on' and continue to introduce themselves or have business cards printed with the prefix or titles such as 'former' President, 'former' General Secretary or 'former' EC member of IWA. Even individuals who had not served within any EC for decades failed to disconnect with or relinquish association with the positions that they once held within the IWA. Henceforth to this day we have innumerable 'former' IWA leaders and EC members who continue this tradition.

IWA Committee featuring (L-R) President Sardul Gill and Piara Khabra (seated) and Late Jaswant Singh Dhami, Darshan Singh Giani, Vishnu Sharma and Surjit Singh Bilga (standing) and other IWA members

IWA Executive Committee, 1972-1977

ANNUAL GENERAL MEETINGS

The Annual General Meetings (AGMs) effectively signalled the start of the race to recruit and mobilise members for the elections of the leadership and control of the IWA. AGMs were routinely tense, chaotic events where incumbent leaders would lock horns with their political challengers intent of dislodging and removing them from office. The formal business to be conducted at the AGMs was always a mere sideshow to the ritual of the verbal duels between incumbent and prospective leaders.

At the AGM, the IWA would announce its entire election process, including dates for opening and closing of membership, members' eligibility to vote, process of nominations of candidates and teams and crucially the election date itself. The quorum for the AGM was 200 or one fifth of its membership, a staggering figure, given that membership usually ran into thousands of members. Many AGMs regularly attracted between 700 to 1,000 members and involved robust debates, constitutional challenges, disruptions and regular bouts of infighting between competing 'factions'.

Each 'faction' would mobilise its own cadres and sympathisers and its 'leader and leading lites' would use the AGM to undermine the credibility of the ruling leadership as well as other opposition groups competing in the elections. It became ritualistic for each and every 'leader' to speak, irrespective of the merits or otherwise of their contributions. This ritual entailed vociferous attacks including accusations of financial mismanagement and impropriety, allegations of unconstitutional actions against the ruling Committee in power and orchestrating tactics to 'grab the microphone' or 'get on to the stage'. Political point scoring, heckling, shouting each together down, constitutional challenges at a level unknown in almost any other organisation was basic 'bread and butter' stuff in these AGMs.

It became a standard practice to give formal notice and advertise the date of AGMs in the local English (Ealing Gazette) and Panjabi (Desh Pardesh) newspapers to ensure that all members were notified and to avoid accusations of undue advantage and subterfuge against ruling Committees. These public notices were essential to counteract any potential legal action on lack of constitutional notifications to members and served to enhance transparency and accountability to the membership.

On completion of the AGM, IWA was preoccupied by and entered a phase of election fever. Membership books, each containing 20 to 25 individual membership forms, would be issued and a membership recruitment campaign conducted over a 6 to 12-week period prior to elections. Individuals interested in contesting elections would begin taking wads of membership books from the IWA offices and vigorously recruit as many members as they could to ensure they were eligible to vote. Hence, most of the membership was recruited within a relatively short time period of around 3 months prior to any forthcoming elections. These membership books along with the membership fees would be deposited at the IWA offices. A membership list would be complied of eligible members and members would be issued with membership cards, which they had to produce as evidence of their membership at the time of voting.

Prior to any elections it was customary for the IWA office to provide information on the total number of members eligible to vote in its elections and issue a membership list to all prospective

IWA Annual General Meeting

IWA members gathering for the Annual General Meeting, Dormers Wells High School

'groups' competing within its elections. These prospective 'groups' would then engage in 'door to door' canvassing and campaigning, hosting their political rallies to mobilise support for their group. Election manifestos though written and available, rarely formed the basis of any clear political strategy, direction or commitments within any group and instead usually focused on issues of mismanagement, unconstitutional actions or lack of integrity of ruling ECs or rival groups.

IWA Annual General Meeting, Featherstone School

IWA members dispersing after Annual General Meeting, Villiers High School

INTERNAL FACTIONS AND ALLIANCES

The aspiration to become elected as an Officer or Ordinary EC member became almost an irresistible and an essential part for any aspiring activist, political or community leader and the number of candidates contesting IWA elections became overwhelming over time.

The development of different clusters of political 'groups' each aligned to or led by a prominent IWA figurehead, ' former IWA leader or leading lite' or aspiring new leader began to emerge. Each such group recruited members, organised and campaigned to get elected and build bigger alliances with other groups to forge teams with a view to contesting and winning elections. From the mid-1960s onwards, different factions, identified by their association with either an existing or 'former' IWA President or General Secretary or their political alignment, became a permanent feature of the politics of the IWA.

Throughout the 1970s and early 1980s, the politics of IWA became synonymous with its leaders as represented by the leaders of its factions that competed in its elections. The most active and dominant factions that actively engaged within the politics of the IWA, included those associated with particular political inclinations such as the communist grouping, the IWA (GB) grouping and the Indian Congress party leaning grouping. Each faction was identified and referred to usually by the name of its President or General Secretary. The main groups competing in the IWA elections have included Broad Alliance, United Front, United Democratic Front, Janata Front and Indian Workers' Front. Invariably the desire to secure a seat as an officer or member of the EC often led to individuals defecting, switching allegiances and 'horse trading' for positions between and within the factions was an accepted and common practice.

One of the most unique and common feature within the election process occurred in the days prior to but particularly on the very day and before the time the nominations by each group was to be formally filed at the IWA Office. Prospective candidates would routinely gather outside the IWA offices at this time. Often amidst frantic scenes, all leaders of different factions along with their key cadres would attend to ensure their teams remained intact and to make deal with other opposing teams, if possible. This last minute 'horse trading' often resulted in some candidates effectively defecting from one group to another, leaving their first group's nomination paper incomplete. This in turn forced that group to make offers of better positions to encourage candidates from competing groups to defect in order that they could complete their own team of 21 candidates and file their election nomination papers. Switching sides and allegiances has been a common feature in the days leading up to the elections as well as in the make-up of IWA groupings and leaderships throughout its history.

This hectic 'horse trading' activity, particularly on the day of close of team nominations for elections, was almost knife edge and resembled the Stock Market trading floor malaise.

Election campaign posters of teams contesting IWA elections

ਅਲਾਇੰਸ ਆਫ਼ ਪ੍ਰੋਗਰੈਸਿਵ ਫੋਰਸਿਜ਼
ALLIANCE OF PROGRESSIVE FORCES
Mr. AVTAR SINGH UPPAL (GENERAL SECRETARY)
Mr. SARDUL SINGH GILL (PRESIDENT)
ELECTION SYMBOL X
ELECTION SYMBOL X
Mr. R.K. PARDESI (VICE PRESIDENT)
Mr. BALRAJ SINGH PUREWAL (ASSTT. GEN. SECY.)
Mr. DEV RAJ BANGAR (FINANCE SECRETARY)
Mr. MUSHTAQ SINGH (CULTURAL SECRETARY)
Mr. GIAN CHAND GAUR (WELFARE SECRETARY)
Mr. PRITAM SIDHU (EDUCATION SECRETARY)
MR. SURINDER SINGH DHILLON (SPORTS SECRETARY)
Mr. DALJIT SINGH GILL (SECY. W/O P'FOLIO)
VOTE FOR
ਸਾਡਾ ਨਿਸ਼ਾਨ ਪੰਜਾ ਹੈ ਇਸ ਤੇ ਨਿਸ਼ਾਨ ਲਾਉਣਾ ਨਾ ਭੁੱਲੋ
ਸਾਡੀ ਅਪੀਲ
17 ਨਵੰਬਰ ਨੂੰ I.W.A ਸਾਊਥਾਲ ਦੀਆਂ ਚੋਣਾਂ ਵਿਚ ਆਪਣੀ ਕੀਮਤੀ ਵੋਟ ਇਸ ਟੀਮ ਨੂੰ ਪਾਕੇ ਕਾਮਯਾਬ ਕਰਾਉ
ਸਾਡੀ ਨੀਤੀ ਅਤੇ ਪ੍ਰੋਗਰਾਮ
Mr. D.S. BOPARAI (GIANI)
Mr. NIRMAL SINGH MAHIL
Mr. BIKKAR SINGH JOHAL
Mr. HARDIAL RANDHAWA
Mr. JAGDEV SINGH SAMRA
Mr. SUKHJIT SINGH WALIA
Mrs. JOGINDER KAUR
Mr. NAZAR SINGH BASRAN
Mr. GURDEEP SINGH SAHOTA
Mr. RESHAM SINGH SAMRA
Mr. GURMEL BRAR

I.W.A. ਦੀਆਂ ਚੋਣਾਂ
ਜਨਤਾ ਫਰੰਟ ਦੇ ਵਿਚਾਰ
ਚੋਣ ਨਿਸ਼ਾਨ ਕਲਾਕ
ਚੋਣ ਨਿਸ਼ਾਨ ਕਲਾਕ

FATEH CHAND BALI VICE PRESIDENT
B.S. DEOL Cllr. CULTURAL SECRETARY
P.S. KHABRA Cllr. PRESIDENT
TARSEM SINGH TOOR GEN. SECRETARY
PRITAM SANDHU FINANCE SECRETARY
SUPPORT ALLIED & VOTE UNITED FRONT
IWA ELECTIONS
SATURDAY THE 17TH NOV 1979
THE HORSE ELECTION SYMBOL X
TARA SINGH SIDHU ASSTT. GEN. SEC
P.S. TAKHAR 'PANKI' WELFARE SEC
GURMAIL DAS EDUCATION SEC.
G.S. DHAMI SPORTS SEC
KARAMJIT SINGH without PORTFOLIO
H.S. RUPRAH
ਸਾਡੀ ਨੀਤੀ ਅਤੇ ਪ੍ਰੋਗਰਾਮ
JAGPAL SINGH KHANGURA
SAWARAN MAHLI
VIRENDERA SHARMA
BUA DAS SHOURIE
AJIT SINGH VIRDEE
SARDUL SINGH BHANDAL
GIAN CHAND SOHI
RAVINDER SINGH JOHAL
PRITAM SINGH BRAR
KULDIP RAI MEHMI

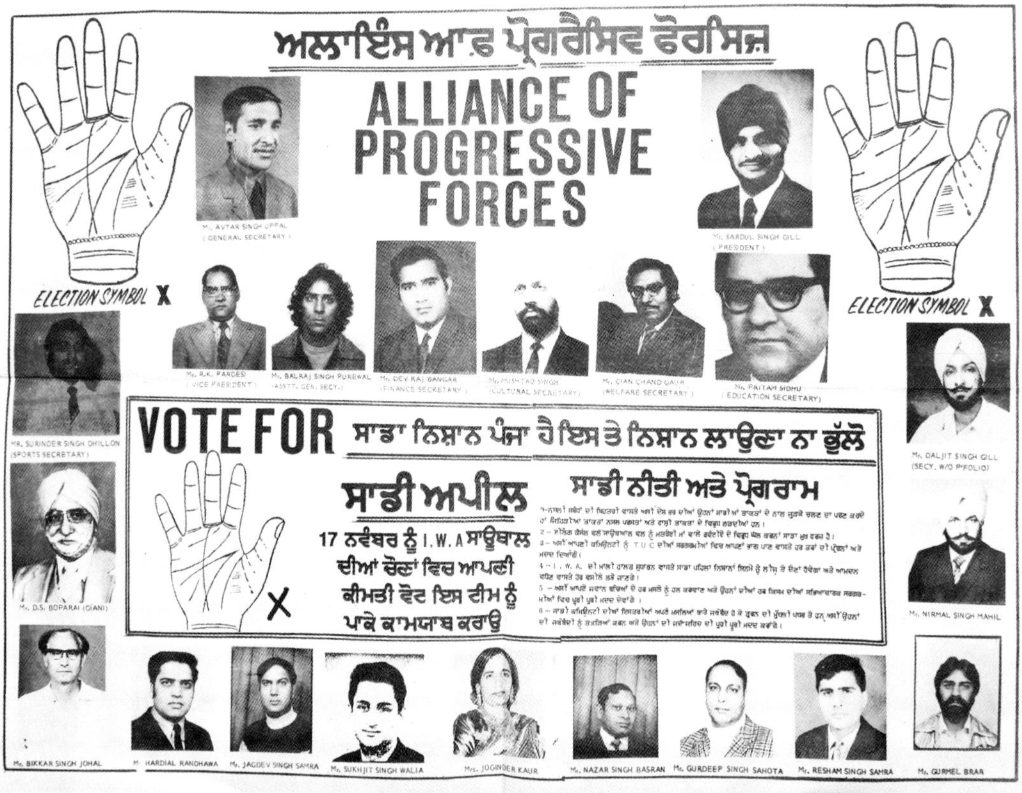

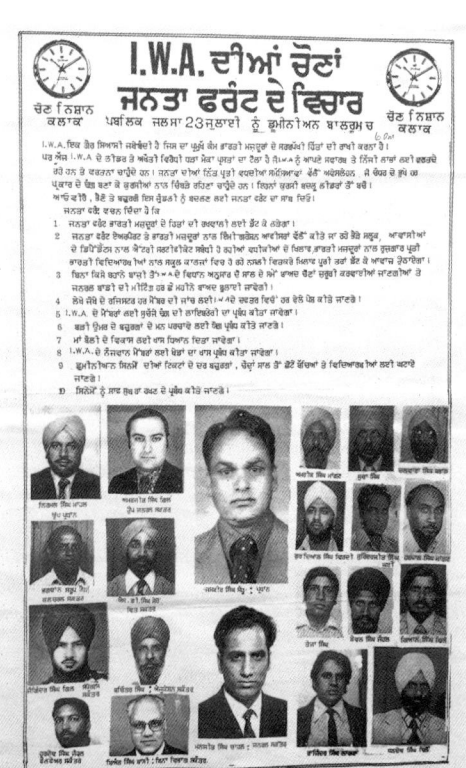

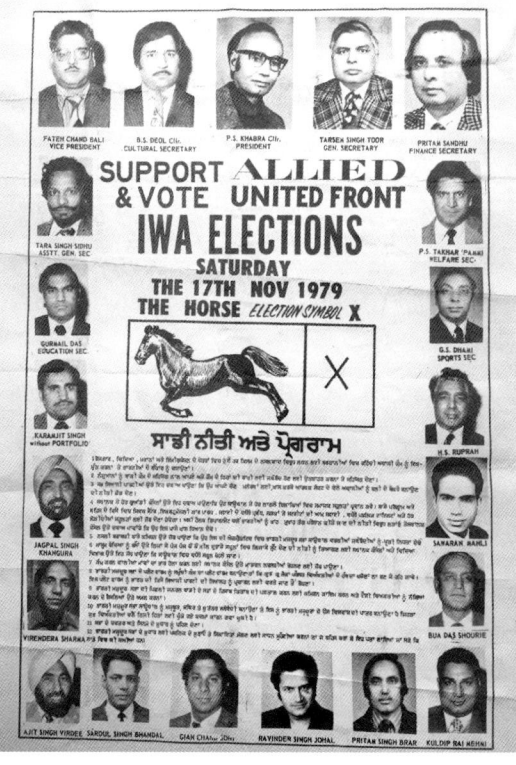

Waiting for outcome of IWA election results, Hounslow Town Hall

ELECTIONS

In its early developmental stages, the IWA election processes and leadership positions were generally amicably agreed arrangements and the desire and need to compete for leadership roles became subservient to the need to support each other to establish the IWA on a strong footing. The influx of Indians in the early 1960s not only resulted in a substantially increased membership base but more critically the arrival of a pool of new aspiring and politically motivated individuals who would inject new life into the body politics of the IWA. Consequently, by 1965 the IWA elections, which were held every 2 years, were to experience their greatest transformation through the political interest and participation generated by these new arrivals.

In the 1968 election, 95 candidates contested the 21 Executive Committee (EC) positions available with an average of 5 candidates standing for each of the 11 different 'Officer' posts and 46 candidates contesting the 10 EC Ordinary member positions. Five parties namely United Front, United Democratic Front, Janata Front, Broad Alliance and Indian Workers' Front, each fielded a team of 21 candidates and elections were conducted through polling booths in 2 local schools.

By the beginning of the 1970s the elections also reached a point where the ballot paper was so long that it became virtually impossible for its voters, many of whom had difficulties in reading English, to find their preferred candidate amongst a huge list of contenders.

During the 1968 to 1970 period, internal legal wrangling resulted in the cancellation of the 1970 election and the incumbent leadership held on until 1972. Even worse, after the 1972 election, Vishnu Dutt along with others who lost that election, challenged the validity of that election result and took the winning team led by Ajit Rai to the High Court. Despite the intention that legal action would force a re-election, legal wrangling resulted in no election taking place at all until 1977.

To deal with allegations of electoral irregularities, impropriety and to ensure fair elections, the IWA contracted and paid the Electoral Reform Society to oversee and supervise all its elections. It also appointed an independent team of 5 non-partisan election scrutineers who were agreed by the contesting teams. The role of these scrutineers was to independently check and verify the validity of the election process, from scrutinising the filing of the nomination papers through to the voting on election day, arbitrating and resolving complaints and disputes between the different contesting factions.

In the November 1979 elections, a total of 108 candidates contested these elections. This included 5 teams each comprising of 21 candidates along with 3 individual candidates who specifically stood for the positions of Vice President, Cultural Secretary and General Secretary. Each of the 5 teams adopted election symbols so that voters could identify their teams and candidates. The symbols of the 5 teams were a Hand, Horse, Telephone, Bow and an Arrow and Tank. The 3 individual candidates contesting these elections used an Elephant and an Eagle as their symbol so that voters could easily identify them on the huge ballot paper.

The IWA responded to this reality of the 'team and grouping' approach and system by changing its electoral process and with effect from its 1983 elections, adopted a system whereby nominations within its elections were only accepted from teams, with each team comprising of

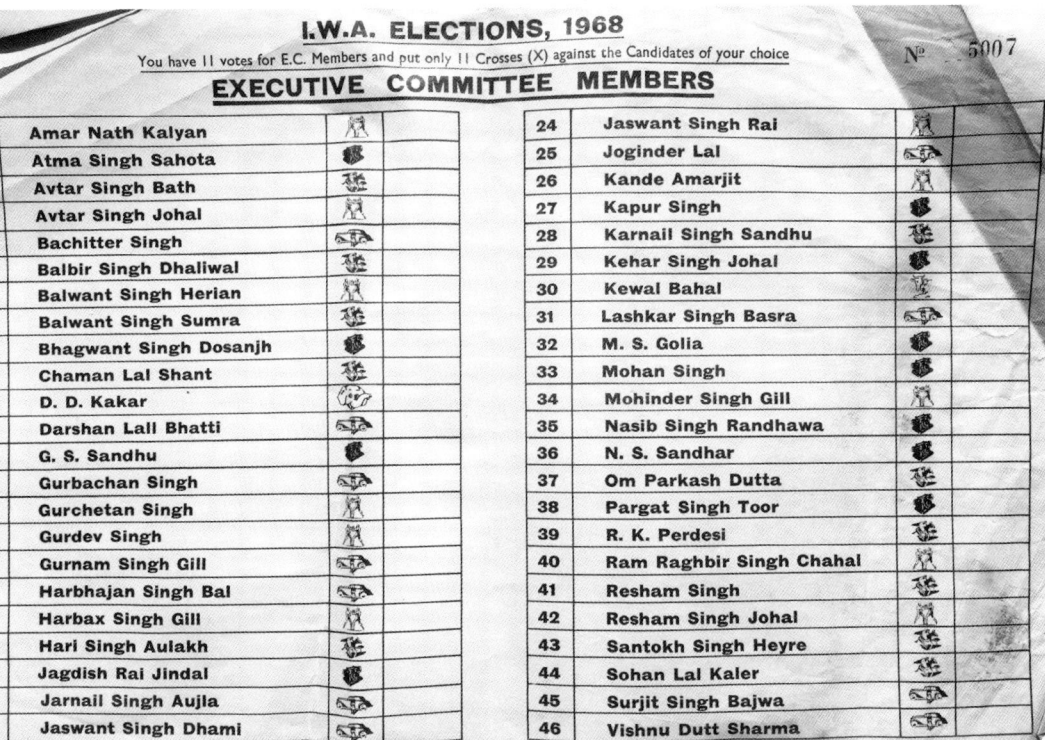

List of candidates for IWA Executive Committee posts, 1968 elections

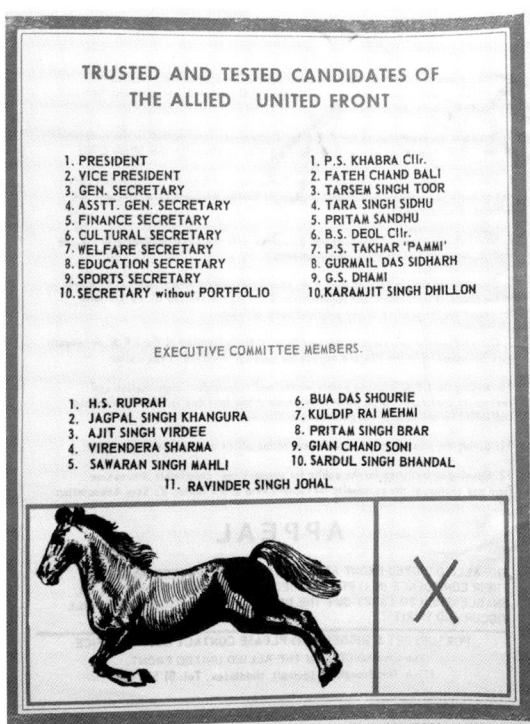

Election campaign poster of Allied United Front team led by Piara Khabra, 1979 elections

21 candidates. This change forced all individuals interested in contesting elections to become a part of a team of 21 and individual nominations were not accepted. The position which any prospective candidate secured within any team depended largely on the numbers of members they had either recruited or could mobilise for their chosen team, along of course with their personal popularity and voter appeal. Some factions on the other hand viewed political inclinations and positions as central determinants to including people into their team.

Until 1989, elections were held every 2 years and the 1989 election was the last time where members actually casted their votes on a ballot paper. In this election, the IWA had a membership of around 16,500 and elections were conducted through 5 polling stations at Villiers High School, Dominion Centre, Ramgharia Hall in Southall, Montague Hall (Hounslow) and in Cranford School. Piara Khabra's team defeated the main rival team, led by Ajit Rai, by just over 3,000 votes.

On 15th July 1989 and under the leadership of Piara Khabra, the IWA constitution was amended to hold elections every 4 years. The principle argument to justify this constitutional amendment was the issue of the huge financial burden on IWA of convening elections every 2 years.

By about 1992 there was effectively no 'ballot election' whereby members physically casted a vote and interest in elections had waned to the extent that no group contested the elections, challenged or stood against the 'Khabra' group which had consolidated a vice- like grip and almost a monopoly on power.

Piara Khabra became elected as Labour MP for Southall in 1992 but also remained President of IWA until his death in 2007. He became the longest serving President in the history of the IWA.

Since 1992 and until 2016 there has been no real 'election', as in the past, where there have been 2 teams competing and where rank and file members actually voted.

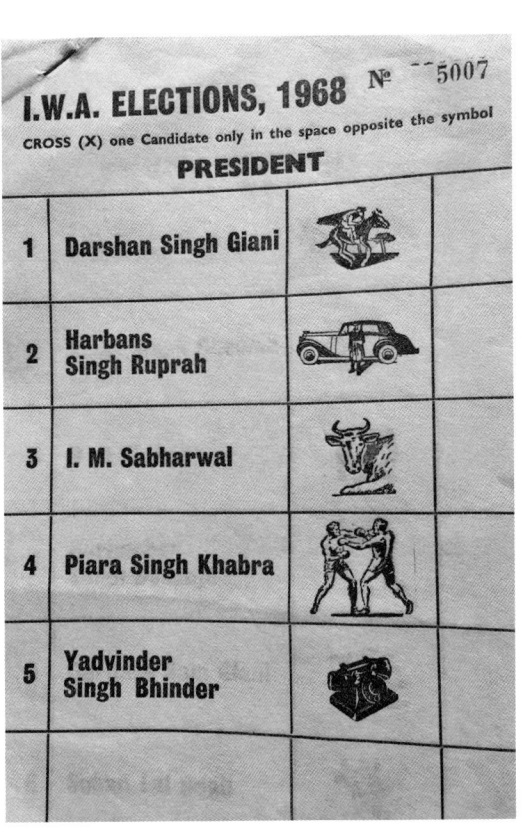

Ballot papers for IWA Executive Committee Officer positions, 1968 elections

ACTIVE OPPOSITION AND DISPUTES

The desire and competition to lead the IWA and occupy its coveted leadership positions fuelled opposition and resentment from unsuccessful teams and individuals defeated through the ballot box. This created a unique situation within the IWA body politics where it led to the development of various 'active opposition groups', each opposing any ruling elected Executive Committee (EC).

Over a period of time an official IWA 'opposition' to any elected leadership evolved and became established, replicating and mirroring the mainstream political system operating in Parliament, where the 'opposition' groups' primary function and role was to make any ruling EC accountable. The 'opposition' groups constantly mobilised IWA members and the wider community against any policy or actions of ruling ECs they deemed detrimental to their own or the community's wider interests. Inevitably this created 'opposition' leaders, positions which themselves became symbolic leadership titles and as such 'coveted' positions in their own right.

The actions of 'opposition' leaders and their groups often led to acrimonious disputes, including legal challenges on constitutional grounds, allegations of corruption, mismanagement, nepotism and cronyism and these became endemic in the body politics of the IWA. During the election period campaigns there was fierce inter-factional infighting with contesting teams circulating propaganda portraying their rivals as untrustworthy, unfit for office, alleging membership irregularities, financial improprieties et al. Different factions would often use cartoons in their propaganda leaflets to depict rivals in unfaltering terms to undermine their rivals' integrity.

Allegations of unconstitutional actions, voting and membership irregularities was a regular feature and a contentious issue for inter-factional infighting and on occasions led to High Court writs. This inevitably led to escalating disputes and political enmity between litigants and in at least 2 cases, contributed to elections not taking place and the incumbent EC holding on to power for a period longer than their elected mandate. On both occasions it created a bizarre situation where the 'opposition' group, which had taken legal action against the incumbent leadership to force it to hold elections, had actually been instrumental to elections being delayed or not taking place after the designated 2-year term.

Election campaign poster of Allied United Front team led by Piara Khabra, 1979 elections

IWA PRESIDENTS AND GENERAL SECRETARIES: 1956 - 2016

Term	President	General Secretary
1957 – 1959	Amar Singh Takhar Jaswant Singh Dhami *	Ajit Singh Rai
1959 – 1961	Jaswant Singh Dhami	Vishnu Dutt Sharma
1961 – 1963	Harbans Singh Ruprah	Vishnu Dutt Sharma
1963 – 1965	Sardul Singh Gill	Piara Singh Khabra
1965 – 1968	Harbans Singh Ruprah	Vishnu Dutt Sharma Tarsem Singh Toor **
1968 – 1970	Darshan Singh Giani	Harjinder Singh Dhillon
1970 – 1972	Darshan Singh Giani	Harjinder Singh Dhillon ***
1972 – 1974	Ajit Singh Rai	Mohinder Singh Padda
1974 – 1977	Ajit Singh Rai	Mohinder Singh Padda ***
1977 – 1979	Vishnu Dutt Sharma	Piara Singh Khabra
1979 – 1981	Piara Singh Khabra	Tarsem Singh Toor
1983 – 1985	Piara Singh Khabra	Tarsem Singh Toor
1985 – 1987	Piara Singh Khabra	Tarsem Singh Toor Balraj Singh Purewal ****
1987 – 1989	Piara Singh Khabra	Jagpal Singh Khangura
1989 – 2007	Piara Singh Khabra	Jagpal Singh Khangura
2007 – 2015	Gurdial Singh Dhami	Tara Singh Sidhu
2016 to date:	Darshan Singh Nagra	Iqbal Singh Vaid

*replaced Amar Singh Takhar who went back to India

**replaced Vishnu Dutt Sharma who resigned to work for JCWI

***elections not held as scheduled and officers continued until elections held

****replaced Tarsem Singh Toor who was murdered

IWA ELECTIONS: Nominated Independent Election Scrutinizers (1):
Mr Frank Day, Dr. Basu, Pritam Singh (Barrister), Jimmy Barzey, Mr.Satish Dhama (Barrister) and Jagdish Sharma.

IWA NOMINATED TRUSTEES OF DOMINION CINEMA*:
Mr. Frank Day, Pargat Singh Toor, Gurchetan Singh Khatra, Mr. Ennals, Dr. P.N. Berry, Mr. Harbans Singh Ruprah and Vishnu Dutt Sharma.

*There were occasional changes to members

PROFILE OF IWA PRESIDENTS AND GENERAL SECRETARIES: 1956-2016

PRESIDENTS:

Amar Singh Takhar
Date of Birth: 1922
Village: Shankar: Jalandhar
Arrival in UK: August 1954
IWA Position(s):
President, 1957-1958
Passed away in 1961

Jaswant Singh Dhami
Date of Birth: August 1920
Village: Dhamian Kalan: Hoshiarpur
Arrival in UK: 1954
IWA Position(s):
President, 1958-1961

Harbans Singh Ruprah
Date of Birth: 14 April 1923
Village: Dhamian Kalan: Hoshiarpur
Arrival in UK: 1954
IWA Position(s):
President, 1961-1963;
    1965-1968

Sardul Singh Gill
Date of Birth: June 1930
Village: Dadupur, Amritsar
Arrival in UK: November 1961
IWA Position(s):
President, 1963- 1965

Darshan Singh Giani
Date of Birth: 15 September 1924
Village: Jathpur: Jalandhar
Arrival in UK: 1963
IWA Position(s):
President, 1968-1972

Ajit Singh Rai
Date of Birth: 21 April 1928
Village: KhanKhana: Nawanshar
Arrival in UK: October 1956
IWA Position(s):
President, 1968-1972
General Secretary, 1957-1959

Vishnu Dutt Sharma
Date of Birth: 19 October 1921
Village: Khatkar Kalan
Arrival in UK: February 1957
IWA Position(s):
President, 1977-1979
General Secretary, 1959-1963
              1965-1968

Piara Singh Khabra
Date of Birth: 20 November 1924
Village: Kaharpur, Hosiarpur
Arrival in UK: 1959
IWA Position(s):
President: 1979-2007
General Secretary, 1963-1965

Gurdial Singh Dhami
Date of Birth: 27 February 1935
Village: Kisanpur: Jalandhar
Arrival in UK: December 1961
IWA Position(s):
President, 2007-2015

Darshan Singh Nagra
Date of Birth: 27 April 1931
Village: Jabbowal
Arrival in UK: 26 December 1961
IWA Position(s): President, 2016

GENERAL SECRETARIES:

Harjinder Singh Dhillon
Date of Birth: 17 April 1935
Village: Dijkot Faislabad (Pakistan)
Arrival in UK: June 1963
IWA Position(s):
General Secretary, 1968-1972

Mohinder Singh Padda
Date of Birth: 1937
Village: Padda, Karpurtla
Arrival in UK: 1962
IWA Position(s):
General Secretary, 1972-1977

Tarsem Singh Toor
Date of Birth: 1933
Village: Jalandhar
Arrival in UK: 1962
IWA Position(s):
General Secreary, 1979-1985

Balraj Singh Purewal
Date of Birth: 3 April 1954
Village: Jassowal: Hosiarpur
Arrival in UK: December 1961
IWA Position(s): General Secretary, 1985

Jagpal Singh Khangura
Date of Birth: 12 May 1937
Village: Latala: Ludhiana
Arrival in UK: 20 March 1963
IWA Position(s):
General Secretary, 1985-2007

Tara Singh Sidhu
Date of Birth: 22 November 1939
Village: Sidam Hari Singh: Jalandhar
Arrival in UK: December 1960
IWA Position(s):
General Secretary, 2007-2015

Iqbal Singh Vaid
Date of Birth: 2 June 1943
Village: Jalandhar
Arrival in UK: 30 March 1963
IWA Position(s):
General Secretary, 2016 to date

IWA WELFARE OFFICERS:

Om Dogra
Date of Birth: 2 May 1933
Village: Bhadsali: Una (Formerly Hosiarpur)
Arrival in UK: 22 October 1961
IWA Position(s): first full-time Welfare Officer, June 1966-June 1969

Krishan Bhatia
Date of Birth: 4 April 1936
Village: Gojra: Lyallpur
Arrival in UK: February 1973
IWA Position(s): Second full-time Welfare Officer, 1974-1981

LONGEST SERVING IWA MEMBER:

Pritam Singh Sandhu
Date of Birth: I October 1940
Village: Rurka Kalan, Jalandhar
Arrival in UK: September 1955
IWA Position(s): Longest serving member, 1956 to date
Finance Secretary/Treasurer, 1977-1997

SECTION 5

This Section provides a summary of IWA's special relationship with Labour Party and the main IWA leaders who spearheaded its efforts to break into mainstream British politics.

BREAKING THE GLASS BARRIERS: From IWA to Mainstream Politics

IWA and Labour Party Connection

The special historical relationship between the IWA and the Labour Party is attributed to a number of factors. The early IWA founding fathers and activists emanated primarily from a socialist or working class background, with varying levels of activism in the struggles for freedom and independence of India. Their early struggles against exploitation within factories brought them into direct contact with the trade union movement, which itself was closely aligned to and an integral part of the Labour Party.

Southall, like many other parts of Britain where early Asian immigrants settled, was historically a working class area politically dominated by the Labour Party. Southall itself had been and continues to be a safe Labour seat since the 1950s. The perception that the Labour Party represented working class interests was perpetuated, internalised and reinforced through a history of working with the trade union movement, which was more receptive to and supportive of the struggles and issues of concern to immigrant communities.

IWA's campaigns to protect immigrant workers' rights, fight unjust and unfair immigration controls and laws, racial discrimination in employment and housing combined with its struggles within the race relations field, formulated some of its understanding of the value and need to engage with mainstream policy and agencies. In the early years this engagement was with the trade union movement and later on it cascaded to the wider political processes.

Given the socialist background of the majority of its leadership and issues affecting its members and wider immigrant communities, the IWA politically aligned itself more with the trade unions and through it with the Labour Party movement. The Conservative party on the other hand became equated and associated with anti-immigration and pro-business policies.

In April 1964, under the leadership of Sardul Singh Gill, the IWA officially backed the Labour Party in the Greater London Council elections on the grounds that *Labour is the party of the working class, because they favour Commonwealth rather than Common Market, and because of their general policies, especially in the field of housing*.

The IWA understood and realised that participation within mainstream political processes and political parties was both essential and critical in its quest to influence mainstream policy and practice, bring about meaningful change and to secure equality and justice for their community in the long term. The growing realisation that Britain was to be their and their children's new permanent home and that they would not be returning back home as envisaged in the 1950s and early 1960s, acted only to further influence IWA to mobilise its leaders and members into mainstream politics. However, racism within and across all the political parties, structures and processes was endemic and acted as a major barrier to the participation of 'coloured' people, irrespective of their political colour. These barriers made change painfully slow but the determination within IWA to break down these barriers and achieve change for themselves and their next generation was equally strong.

The Labour Party was politically assessed to be the most appropriate and effective political

Indian Independence Day Celebration rally featuring (L-R) Sidney Bidwell MP, Ajit Rai, Micheal Foot (leader of Labour Party), Manjit Singh, K. Kanwal

IWA leaders and members with Tony Benn MP

mechanism to facilitate entry into mainstream political power. By the mid-1960s, IWA leaders began to strategically place themselves within local Labour Party wards in Southall, by joining and recruiting Asians who were by then becoming significant in number, particularly in some wards in Southall such as Northcote, The Broadway and Glebe wards. The IWA leaders mobilised the IWA political machinery, membership along with their traditional extended family, village and kinship ties to recruit members into Labour Party. Simultaneously their political awareness and astuteness informed them that on the basis of their links, composition of the local constituency and wards which had increasing Asian populations and were traditionally Labour strongholds, they were strategically placed to take the first steps into mainstream politics.

In May 1968, Sardul Gill, one of the IWA Presidents, using IWA as a base, prepared the ground and took the historical first step, smashing the glass ceiling of racial discrimination, to become the first elected Asian Councillor in Southall, inspiring and trail blazing the way for others to follow.

Over time the IWA's political strategy, recruitment drive, community base and mobilisation of the Asian electorate and its own membership targeted the local Labour Party and these factors combined to make it possible and indeed 'normal' for Asians to be nominated and elected as Councillors, not only in Southall but in Hounslow as well. Using this multi-faceted strategy, Asian candidates linked to the IWA, overcome the racial discrimination within the Labour Party, paved the way and set the parameters for other Asian communities and politicians to follow.

An extraordinary moment in politics occurred when Labour Party was overwhelmingly defeated by the Conservatives in Ealing Council elections with the exception of Southall wards, which remained solidly Labour. 15 Asian Labour Councillors from Southall effectively provided the 'majority opposition' to the Tory controlled Council.

Another extraordinary moment in British Asian political history was simmering and about to take place. In 1992, Piara Singh Khabra, President of IWA would emerge as MP for Southall Ealing.

'Over the decades the IWA acted as a training nursery for a generation of Black and Asian community leaders and inspired and harnessed Asian community leadership'.
Cllr. Ranjit Dheer JP: 2015

Piara Khabra addressing public meeting at Dominion cinema with Manjit Litt (L)

SARDUL GILL: First Elected Asian Councillor in Ealing, May 1968

Sardul Gill became active in the IWA from the time he arrived in Britain and in 1965 was elected as its President. A powerful political speaker, he was the first Sikh to become politically active in the local Labour Party.

In 1968, the former President of IWA, Sardul Singh Gill, became the first elected Asian Labour Party Councillor in Southall. Sardul Gill was elected for a term of 3 years in May 1968 and his election marked a political watershed. His election acted as a catalyst and served to give a generation of IWA representatives and activists a new confidence to enter mainstream politics.

Sardul Gill became a prominent and national Labour Party figure and made an impassioned speech at the Labour Party Conference in 1969. By the late 70s, Sardul Gill became the leading contender to dethrone the sitting Labour MP, Sidney Bidwell as MP for Southall Ealing, a feat he was unable to accomplish despite a number of challenges.

'Southall was the turban of England'

'We did not have 'chips on our shoulders' that we were black, that we were discriminated against. Persuasion was our slogan.

We did not bulldoze or hit back

Innumerable white people were part of the common struggle of our community.

Because our fight was not against white people but against prejudice'.
   Sardul Gill: 1992

VISHNU SHARMA: The Independent Candidate, 1973 Council Elections

Vishnu Dutt Sharma was an ardent and lifelong communist who on the second day of his arrival in Britain searched for the offices of the Communist Party of Britain and became its member.

Vishnu Sharma, though educated and versed in Indian politics, did not speak any English and on arrival in Britain immersed himself in learning English and became the first member of the Executive Committee of the Communist Party of Great Britain.

In 1973, Vishnu Sharma stood as an Independent candidate in the local Council elections in Northcote Ward, Southall. He lost to a Labour Councillor, who had held his seat for 24 years and had been a previous Mayor of Southall, by only 23 votes. This was a testimony to Vishnu Sharma's political commitment, extraordinary popularity and standing within the local community. In equal measure it illustrated the community and political base and force that IWA could generate for its prominent leaders and activists.

Vishnu Sharma was one of the few 'national' political figures who emerged out of the IWA which provided him a critical platform to reach this nexus.

PIARA KHABRA: First Asian Member of Parliament for Southall/Ealing, May 1992

This ultimate political aspiration and dream of the Asian community was to turned into a reality by Piara Singh Khabra, President of IWA, who became a Member of Parliament for Southall/Ealing constituency in May 1992.

Piara Khabra, as President of IWA strategically used the IWA community base and reputation to build his political campaign to become a MP, recruiting and strategically using the second generation of young activists such as Balraj Purewal into the IWA leadership and combining these activists with the older IWA and constituency members he had recruited and consolidated over his political life to fulfil his personal as well as the community's final political quest and aspiration.

The campaign to become an MP was to be fraught with difficulties, including the pressure from the central Labour Party machinery whose new priorities focused more on inclusion of women candidates. Simultaneously the rise of 'Black Sections' within the Labour Party, which favoured inclusion of black candidates in shortlisting of MPs, also posed challenges for a local community candidate. The final hurdle was to overcome the challenge from the sitting MP of 23 years who had strong support from the trade unions affiliated to the Labour Party.

In spite of these challenges, Piara Khabra with massive logistical and political support from the IWA, was elected as MP for Southall/Ealing constituency and replaced the sitting MP, Sidney Bidwell.

Piara Khabra served as an MP from 1992 until his death in 2007 and paved the way for Virendra Sharma, who in the mid -1970s had also served as a member of the IWA Executive Committee to replace him as MP.

Piara Khabra was the longest serving IWA President in the history of IWA and transformed the political vision, aspiration and dream of having the first elected Asian MP in Southall, nurtured by the IWA leadership for decades, into a reality.

IWA EXECUTIVE COMMITTEE MEMBERS WHO BECAME COUNCILLORS

By the mid-1970s, the demographics within most of Southall's electoral wards had changed significantly and the local constituency and electorate became overwhelming of Asian origin. Within this framework the IWA leadership continued its political strategy of actively enrolling membership into the local Labour Party. The Conservative Party in contrast attracted little attention form the IWA leadership but nevertheless local Asians starting taking interest and becoming its members as well.

In recognition of IWA's powerful political base, it became customary for aspiring local Asian politicians to seek its patronage and align them with the IWA leadership, in order to get nominated and elected as local ward councillors. IWA's Executive Committee (EC) members, past and present, similarly utilised the Association to promote their personal political interests and to gain a foothold in politics and to become local Councillors.

The IWA's massive membership base, which at its peak comprised of nearly 22,000 members (circa 1985), with elections held every 2 years and attracting up to 10,000 voting members along with its formidable electioneering and campaigning experience, machinery and networks and wider community base, made it the dominant political force in Southall.

Throughout the 1970s and 1980s, holding the position of an Officer or an Ordinary member of the IWA EC, was seen as a more prestigious and powerful political position than that of being an elected local councillor.

Over the decades a number of IWA EC members became elected as Labour councillors in Ealing including: Sardul Gill, Bhagwan Deol, Virendra Sharma, Piara Khabra, Ram Kishan Perdesi, Bachittar Sahota, Tej Ram Bagha, Tejinder Dhami, Mohinder Midha.

IWA EC members elected as Labour councillors in Hounslow have included: Jagpal Khangura, Harbaksh Khangura, Harbans Kanwal, Gopal Dhillon, Mohinder Gill.

Piara Khabra became MP for Southall in 1992.

Gurcharan Singh stood as Conservative Party Candidate for MP in Ealing/Southall constituency in 2010 and in Slough constituency in 2015.

Many others who stood for or were elected as local councillors for various political parties were associated directly with or had links with the IWA or its leadership.

IWA Executive Committee, 1977-1979

IWA Executive Committee, 2007

IWA: THE LEGACY

The struggles of the founding fathers of the IWA and their predecessors have made Southall what it is today, an icon within the Asian community nationally and internationally and within Britain generally.

The IWA's political discourse was an unequivocal commitment to secular values, mass community and worker participation which inter-linked to turn its concept 'of the people and for the people' into a living and thriving reality. These also became it most distinguishable hallmarks, as members of the community, who were not even its members, felt they had a stake and a real say in the running of the organisation, and the organisation in turn reciprocated by taking up their issues and causes.

When Southall speaks the country listens.

The IWA's political legacy, leading to its Presidents elected as the first Asian Councillor and culminating in its President being elected as the MP for Southall, inspired a new generation of Asian and African-Caribbean leaders into mainstream politics across the country.

From its humble beginning, IWA Southall emerged as one of the most influential and largest Indian organisation in Britain of people from the Indian diaspora and outside of India, with over 22,000 paid members at its peak. The fact that successive Indian government representatives, including Prime Ministers of India, visited or met with IWA delegations, is a testimony to its status as a genuine representative and voice of people from the Indian diaspora and its international standing and influence.

In the early 1970s, IWA became an organisation generating an income of tens of thousands of pounds annually from its Dominion Cinema, membership fees and donations.

Today, the IWA owns the freehold of the entire former Dominion Cinema site, which it has leased to London Borough of Ealing for 99 years since 1983 and which currently occupies the Southall Library and the Dominion Arts and Cultural Centre.

The IWA further owns its own freehold 3 story building adjacent to the Dominion Centre which houses its offices. In addition, it owns a small car park at the rear of the Dominion Centre. In 2016, the IWA is in the process of negotiating a deal to sell its Car Park area to a property developer for £850,000.

The IWA assets are estimated to be worth at least £3 million at 2016 rates.

The future generation of IWA leaders are set to inherit a multi-million pound organisation.

The early IWA pioneers and their survivors pass the mantle, the quest for equality and dignity, a just and fair society, to the next generation. Do not ever forget them and their struggles.

My name is Balraj Singh Purewal
My name is everything.
It defines my gender, my faith, my language.
It locates the geographical area in Panjab my family originates from.

I am because we are. Because we are therefore I am.

I salute the founding members of IWA and all those who struggled, including our parents so that we could have a better future.

SECTION 6

This section lists the key milestones in the history of IWA.

KEY MILESTONES IN THE HISTORY OF IWA

1956
Movement to begin formation of Bharti Mazdoor Sabha (Indian Workers' Association: Southall) begins.
IWA founding members holds weekly social activity for Indian community at Southall Community Centre, Bridge Road, Southall.
Amar Singh Takhar becomes first IWA President.

1957
IWA delegation meets Jawarlal Nehru, Prime Minister of India, in London on issue of irregular immigration status of Indians in Britain.
3rd March 1957: Inaugural Meeting of IWA Southall.

1958
Chief Minister of Panjab, Darbara Singh, speaks at first IWA Annual Conference at Southall Community Centre attended by 400 people.
Amar Singh Takhar re-elected as IWA President and Ajit Singh Rai elected as General Secretary.
18 October 1958: IWA hosts farewell party for Amar Singh Takhar, who leaves Britain to go back to Panjab permanently.
Jaswant Singh Dhami becomes IWA President.

1959
Jaswant Singh Dhami continues as IWA President.

1960
6th May 1960: Jawarlal Nehru, Prime Minster of India, visits UK and meets IWA delegation regarding regularisation of status of Indians without proper Indian passports and documentation.

1961
Harbans Singh Ruprah elected as IWA President.

1962
IWA campaigns against first Immigration Act 1962.
IWA supports Asian workers strike at Rockware Glass factory, Greenford.

1963
Sardul Singh Gill elected as IWA President.

1964
IWA purchases 18 Featherstone Road, Southall and sets up a Welfare Centre and offices.
IWA coordinates and acts as Lead member in setting up CARD, a national umbrella organisation to campaign and influence Government to legislate against racial discrimination.
IWA supports Asian workers strike at Dura Tube and Wire Ltd, Feltham.

1965
Harbans Singh Ruprah re-elected as President.
December 1965: IWA purchases Dominion Cinema for £75,000 raising £25,000 from members and local community.
IWA starts showing Indian films at Dominion Cinema.
IWA launches campaign against racist policy of dispersal and 'Bussing' of Asian schoolchildren in Southall.

1966
IWA supports the Asian workers' strike at R. Woolfe's Rubber Factory (Southall) and organises unionisation of its Asian workforce.

1967
Joint Council for the Welfare of Immigrants

(JCWI), a national body campaigning on immigration, nationality and asylum issues set up in Dominion Cinema with Vishnu Sharma as its co-founder.

Vishnu Sharma relinquishes position of IWA General Secretary to join JCWI as a paid worker.

1968

Sardul Singh Gill, ex-IWA President, elected as the first Asian Councillor in Ealing Council in May elections.

Darshan Singh Giani elected as IWA President.

8 May 1968: IWA founder member, Jaswant Singh Dhami, passes away.

1969

January 1979: Indira Gandhi, Prime Minister of India, visits and addresses IWA Conference at Dominion Cinema and meets IWA leadership.

1970

Bi-annual IWA elections postponed.

1972

Ajit Rai elected as President.

IWA coordinates support in the resettlement of British Asians expelled from Uganda under the dictatorship of Idi Amin.

1973

IWA leaders present petition to 10 Downing Street and participates in national demonstration against immigration Act 1973.

IWA successful in its campaign for the regularisation of illegal immigrants and Government announces Amnesty for Commonwealth citizens and citizens of Pakistan with effect from 1 January 1974.

1975

IWA delegation led by Ajit Rai visits EEC commissioners as part of IWA's campaign against British entry into EEC

25 November 1975: IWA delegation meets Indira Gandhi, Prime Minister of India and Indian Ministers, regarding the Emergency imposed by Indian Government in India and attend International Conference Against Fascism held in Patna, India.

1976

IWA organises mass community mobilisation in memory of the death of Gurdip Chaggar, killed on 4th June 1976 in Southall.

1977

137 candidates including 5 teams, each comprising of 21 candidates, contest IWA elections.

Janata Front Group led by Vishnu Sharma and Piara Khabra wins IWA elections.

IWA begins to face financial problems due to loss of income from its Dominion cinema.

1978

IWA membership reaches 13,000 members.

1979

January 1979: IWA exposes and campaigns against 'Virginity' testing of Asian women at Heathrow airport and sends delegation to Indian Government.

IWA leads community opposition and organises a March to Ealing Town Hall to protest against meeting of National Front (NF) in Southall Town Hall on 23 April 1979

IWA sets up a Defence Campaign and Fund in support of the 342 people arrested and charged in the community protests against the NF meeting of 23 April 1979.

Piara Khabra elected as IWA President.

IWA membership reaches a peak of 22,500.

IWA debt increases to £80,000.

1981
Dominion Cinema ceases to function and is closed.
IWA financial debt increases to £120,000.

1982
23rd December: IWA leases Dominion Cinema to Ealing Council for 99 years. Council repays all IWA's debts, agrees to build new independent building for IWA and pays IWA £50,000 as part of this deal.

1983
IWA temporarily relocates its Welfare service and office to Southall Town Hall.
Team voting system introduced in IWA elections.
Piara Khabra re-elected as IWA President.
Dominion Cinema building demolished.

1985
IWA organises first 3 day Anti-Racism Training Programme for public sector professionals.
IWA manage 3 Manpower Services Commission funded projects employing around 36 staff.
IWA membership 8,000

1986
July 1986: Tarsem Singh Toor, IWA General Secretary, murdered.
IWA Welfare service and office relocate to its permanent new building at 112 The Green, Southall.

1987
IWA secures first grant for post of Community Development Officer from Ealing Council
IWA launches its first publication: *Regeneration of Racism: Hypocrisy of Inner City Policies* produced by a Collective run by Tuku Mukherjee.

IWA membership 16,500

1988
January 1988: Neil Kinnock MP: Leader of Labour Party visits IWA Offices and opens the new Dominion Arts and Community Centre.
IWA secures grant for post of Community Development Officer from Hounslow Council and opens an IWA Office at 10 School Road, Hounslow.

1989
Piara Khabra re-elected as President.
IWA national conference on Dual Indian Nationality held at Dominion Centre.
15 July 1989: IWA constitution amended to hold elections every 4 years.

1990
IWA campaigns against Poll Tax.

1991
IWA membership 17,000

1992
Piara Khabra: IWA President, elected as first Asian MP of Southall Ealing constituency.
Death of Vishnu Sharma, founder member and IWA President while attending a conference in India.
1992 - 2007: Piara Khabra continues as President of IWA.

1996
IWA supports striking workers at Hillingdon Hospital

2007
19 June: Death of Piara Singh Khabra.

2016
IWA in process of negotiating sale of its Car Park to Property Developer for an estimated £850,000

ACKNOWLEDGEMENTS

I wish to acknowledge the contribution of Heritage Lottery Fund, which funded a project to record and preserve the history of the IWA for future generations and which included the production of a documentary film on the history and work of the IWA. My involvement in this important project encouraged me to write this book.

I wish to acknowledge the contribution and support of the many current and past members of the IWA Executive Committee as well as many members particularly Surjit Singh Bilga, Tara Singh Sidhu, Gurdial Singh Dhami, Pritam Singh Sandhu, Resham Singh Samra and many early settlers in Southall and their survivors for their ongoing support to my efforts in writing this book.

I particularly wish to thank Baljit Ruprah-Shah, Sukhindra Singh Rai, Darshan Singh Giani's family and all the other colleagues and friends who provided valuable information and access to materials to make this book possible.

I wish to thank my friend, Suresh Grover, for his continuing moral support to me.

Last but not least I am indebted to the encouragement and support from The Asian Health Agency which provided me financial support, enabling this book to be printed and published.

Balraj Purewal

REFERENCES

Joginder Shamsher Singh: *Panjabis in Britain: 1958*

Hansard: 1803 -2205: 18 February 1968

The Middlesex Gazette and County Times: 1 March 1958

Smith and Marmo: *Uncovering Virginity Testing: Gender and History: April 2011*

Desai, 1963:105; Aurora, 1967:45

Indian Workers' Association and IWA Annual Reports

Maurice Kogan: *Dispersal in the Ealing Local Education Authority Schools' System:* Report to Race Relations Board, 1976

John, De Witt: *Indian Workers' Association in Britain* (Oxford University Press, 1969)

British Sikh Report- *An Insight into British Sikh Community:* P. Bance

Aldridge, John (November 1999)

Interview with Vishnu Dutt Sharma by Dave Cook

Past IWA Executive Committee and other members

Wikipedia

Labour Heritage: Bulletin: Autumn 2004

Olivier Esteves

The National Archives

PHOTOGRAPHS

Photographs are primarily by courtesy of Harbans Singh Ruprah family, Ajit Singh Rai family, Darshan Singh Giani family, Surjit Singh Bilga, Resham Singh Samra and IWA offices.

Other photographs are by courtesy of Gunnerbury Park Museum, London Borough of Ealing Library Service, Tower Hamlets Local History Library & Archive.

I wish to sincerely acknowledge and thank them all for their support work and contributions.